I have been the bad guy:
Neuroqueer Self-Realizations
in the Algorithmic *Envirusment*

ISBN: 978-1088266410
Published by IngramSpark

Cover designed using Nightcafe & Canva

Printed in United States

First Edition

Table of Contents

Acknowledgements

For every direct speaking, substance abusing,
violated autist of a family who didn't understand.
Thank you for surviving to this day, and for who
you have been every day. We deserve(d) better.

Introduction.

Most everything you are about to read I have hidden about myself from the world for thirty years. ("No one is going to believe you, Dr. bird." "No one is going to trust what you have to say about your own life.") What I'm about to tell you are my experiences of having lived my entire life in my own body. The ways how, from living my life in my own body, I only knew what I knew, everything became normal in repetition, and how I realized everything was connected.

Throughout this memoir, I write in my unmasked natural speaking style. If you don't like that, you are welcome to read someone else's memoir. This one is mine, so take my voice, or leave it.

With that said, consider this introduction a broad reaching trigger warning for discriminations, abuse, and sexual violences because my having hid these parts of myself did not protect me from them. I am well aware, as someone who was told by my therapist not to seek a professional diagnosis "because it would hurt me more than it would help me," that sharing these parts of myself that I have kept hidden, put me in real danger of being hated and/or further systemically discriminated against for the entire rest of my life. Especially, as I write this in the U.S.

eugenics context that has emerged since COVID-19 started, and because of the fascism that has returned.

I am accepting the risks I take in deciding to share this memoir style version of my life, for two reasons: 1) to revisit my life and accept myself for the strong, imperfect, and vulnerable human I know myself to be, as well as 2) for anyone and everyone who disclosed to me that they believe reading my book will help them -- in whatever capacity that may be -- because of my TikToks.

This is not, and could never be, the exhaustive retelling of my life. It is however main memories retold about my life, as I remember living. I have chosen to include no names besides my own. I let the actions of others speak for themselves, in relation with my own. I have not been a perfect person [insert that one Hoobastank song]. But seriously. Most people who lived in my immediate vicinity will probably not believe most, if not all, of what I'm about to disclose herein because of the way that they perceived me as life happened. And the sheer gravity of it all. So, let me make one thing clear before I proceed: If you don't believe me, it doesn't matter. I Couldn't Care Less. Since you haven't lived my life in my body, you're not an authority on describing my neurotype.

Even if readers gain nothing else from reading this retelling of my life, they should be able to still walk away with a better understanding of why my boundaries are now so strong, I block so swiftly on social media, and refuse to conform to certain social norms if/when they demand me to sacrifice my own authenticity. At the absolute minimum, readers will walk away with a better understanding *how* and *why* there are ongoing massive neuroqueer self-realizations happening, that have exploded in algorithmic spaces (like TikTok), especially post-March 2020. I mention that in this work because my dissertation was about sociosexual ecologies in the algorithmic age, and halfway through writing that, C19 hit. That, and the fact I am a late-in-life realized autistic person myself, are the reasons one of the major findings of my project was the neuroqueer self-realizations in the algorithmic age on platforms like TikTok. If neither of those things happened, I would be as painfully unaware, and suppressed, as I was before starting my PhD. And as you'll see, there is a chance that I wouldn't be alive to say anything, if the pandemic hadn't happened.

My experience does not, and could never, represent all neuroqueer autists (a word I use to describe myself, that non-autists aren't welcome to use, and not all autistic people resonate with or choose to identify with, and I respect that) or all late-in-life realized autists. Our community is not a hivemind. Many of us, however, have exchanged solidarity regarding many similarities during the most connected time in human history and it has changed the entire course of our lives. For more of my life than not, I have been the bad guy, and it didn't have to be this way.

I have chosen to organize this book into three parts: Lil' bird, Bern'd Out, and Dr. bird. Included at a key point in each chapter is one of my poems, that speak to a theme of that point in my life.

As such, the first two chapters, especially, recount oppressive norms, as well as many survived incidents of sexual violence, social struggles, and substance abuse, revisited as totally normal events of my life because, as an unrecognized autist, these we/are "normal" occurrences. For these reasons, and more, within these chapters, I have chosen to warn readers with !!!s right before any passages in which I explicitly detail systemic violences, so they can make a decision.

Whenever you reach those points in any chapter, if you are not in the mental space to read any specified content, instead, please, either: 1) pause and take time for yourself instead of doing so, and/or 2) know that I have anticipated this, and installed a measure to accommodate anyone who cannot or should not read accounts of these natures. For such readers, I have installed a system throughout, using symbols. Meaning, right after any passage with graphic violence mentioned, I also indicate that the particularly violent details are over, by placing 7 rows of

s. Then, as the chapter resumes after those yellow symbols, I have done my best to describe basic relevant info, still allowing readers to comprehend as close to the full context of what happened as possible. I know there is no way to create a "safe space" for anyone in a world as inequitable and violent as this. My hope is by implementing these measures, it will reduce harm, while sharing my story as an oppressive participant in and/or survivor of various systemic violences normalized in the U.S.

Within chapter one, I define "neuroqueer," as coined by Dr. Nick Walker in her work, followed by introducing readers to secrets of my childhood and teenage years, recounting behaviors and habits that, as I was raised, both my family and passing friends, implicitly and explicitly, taught me to "kept to myself" or eliminate. To them, I appeared to be an awkward, selfish, and often aggravated child who had outbursts at seemingly tiny things. I was seen as having a "short fuse" who was acting ungrateful for what I had. This led others to cast me as the "bad guy". In other words, for being autistic, I was both disciplined and bullied for existing as my whole self. This abusive treatment catalyzed me to undergo extreme forms of full body-mind micromanagement. This was the point in my life where I learned that my personality, feelings, emotions, and needs were not only not desirable to accept by loved ones but were also too much for alleged friends. I quickly learned that to make myself tolerable to others, I needed to cater to and follow their lead. Near the end, I explain how as a teen, I met a "friend" who made racist "jokes", and since I learned to mimic others to survive, I then took part in casual racisms framed as "jokes", revealing a lesser-spoken-about cycle of violence, due to "matrices of domination" (Patricia Hill Collin's term for the way interrelated domains organize societal power relations). I believe this awful "normal" disclosure will add to existing knowledge about autistic racisms, nuancing what is known by Black / ethnic studies / whiteness studies scholars, among others. I end by differentiating between being *the bad guy* and choosing to become "the bad guy" instead.

That distinction sets the stage for understanding the rest of my pre-thirty-year-old life. Within chapter two, I take readers through a temporal autopsy of my flesh wounds that further explicate what I have called the "sexually violent U.S ecology," that exemplifies many common ways that (as is extensively documented in research studies from the last fifteen years) autists are at risk for significantly higher rates of being pervasively discriminated against for existing (both inside and outside of work), substance abuse, sexual violence(s), self-harm, and suicidality, than non-autistics.

With that said, this was the hardest chapter to write and will be the hardest chapter to read by far. I would recommend you do not read the entire chapter in one sitting. It may be too much to hold. The same reason it was hard to read / write is because these violences are so pervasively normal. We're only at the beginning of lost generations of autists coming forward who've survived these often-interplaying harms, and my hope is that disclosing my own will add to recent realizations. (This chapter is best read and understood in tandem with my "Requirement Politics" article on my Academia page/out soon.)

In chapter three, after a brief discussion of my experience of therapy and therapist's reactions to me throughout my life, the first section is about "when I thought I could work/drink it all away". Then, I talk readers through my early to mid-twenties, and an autistic script I have often repeated when people ask me how I stumbled, luckily, into my communication master's program with an extended part I always leave out about the time at the end where I was attacked by pure evil. After surviving my quick brush with death (and Robin Williams died R.I.P), I explain how the mentors at this point in my life helped me rebuild my self-esteem and sense of identity from the ground up at the age of 23. As becomes clear, even with a handful of cool people supporting me throughout that process, it was still rough, and thus not entirely pretty or flattering, due to my unknown alexithymia, substance abuse to cope with social overstimulation, and interoception issues. I, then, describe a particular point at which due to autistic Bern' out, (bad ol') compulsory heterosexuality, and confusion, I mistook loving the way someone loved me for loving him back, which slipped me back into be *the bad guy* territory. This was followed by a fuller more abrupt series of events (or animorph, if you [other 90s babies] will) from being seen as *the bad guy* into choosing to instead live as "the bad guy". I also uncover some ways my shift was complicated because, obviously, living categories of self are never as cut and dry as words make them seem.

Readers may notice final two chapters are significantly shorter than the first three because that's just how it went down. For anyone who may've just looked at the page count of chapter four and thought, "What are you taking about? It looks like chapter four is pretty fucking long" First, I respect that. Also, it's only long because it includes a fuck ton of screenshotted tweets from 2020. The vast majority of what is long about the chapter is due to the space they comprise. For the fullest picture, readers should also read my three columns that I wrote to the BGSU newspaper around that time: 1) "Six Questions for BGSU Community Consideration..." 2) "Higher Education Attacks in Silence" and 3) "Lifting Mask Mandates is 'Irresponsible". I end this chapter by discussing my own grieving and self-realization process in the *envirusment*.

Then, after 33 years, it's 📓☕🎵closing time. Unlike a good bar DJ paid to signal closure with that one overplayed song at most bars, I close my memoir about these first 33 years of my life by challenging readers to think about the vast implications of our well-documented loneliness and touch hunger epidemic, the sex apocalypse, and the implications of the fucking fact that mass self-realizations are happening on platforms in the ongoing (systemically denied) *envirusment*. (Although some readers may be drunk on [long-]COVID-19 denialism, you'll want to read this.)

Part One.
Lil' bird

Chapter One. Who Am I? The Bad Guy.

My name is Dr. Bernadette "bird" Bowen. My mom named me after Saint Bernadette because she was volunteering at a church nearby and saw a poster with the church by the same name on it. She always said if she ever had "another girl" she'd name them Bernadette. That, the holiness, maturity, and professionalism of my first name never sat right with me, so I mainly go by "bird".

I was born with multiple hernias that had to be removed and were also hardly spoken of again. I was assigned female at birth in the United States, and therefore, I was assigned to be ashamed of my body and myself from the day I was born. I am a millennial, and I am not a woman. I am a non-binary (enby) neuroqueer person. Dr. Nick Walker, first in her 2008 essay coining the term, as well as in her book *Neuroqueer Heresies,* and on her website defines "neuroqueer" as both a verb, "neuroqueering as the practice of queering (subverting, defying, disrupting, liberating oneself from) neuronormativity and heteronormativity simultaneously" and, that can also be an adjective "serv[ing] as a label of social identity. One can neuroqueer, and one can *be* neuroqueer. A neuroqueer individual is any individual whose identity, selfhood, gender performance, and/or neurocognitive style have in some way been shaped by their engagement in practices of neuroqueering, *regardless of what gender, sexual orientation, or style of neurocognitive functioning they may have been born with*". Long before I knew what autism is/was (or had the language to know I'm a neuroqueer enby), for most of my life, I was mistaken for someone else.

Yellow

After
A week

Of This
World,

I turned
Yellow.

My liver's
Formal
Proclamation:

"Your
Breastmilk

Is No Good
Here."

I do not
Nourish

Like
the rest
Of you.

If you
Try To
force me,

My filters
Malfunction.

We are not
Compatible
Devices.

Stop trying
to fit
us together.

Let me be.

Shortly after I was born, my mom's attempting to breast-feed me gave me jaundice. Luckily, my mom's favorite color was yellow. Maybe that's why she called me "Lil' bird". She also said I had a very hard time letting go of my pacifier as a toddler. My mom used to tell me I'd "make a good lawyer because I love to and am good at arguing". In my early life, I was very confident in my ability to share information and help people. Turns out many parents do not like to, or don't believe they have anything to, learn from a child. Like, my mom always wanted me to wear dresses, and I hated dresses. The one picture she always kept on her dresser was of a little me, probably about 6 or 7 years old, in a dress she picked out with plastic beaded jewelry on. It was like she'd frozen in time a femininity-clad version of me because that's how she preferred me.

My older sister played that role for her. She played Barbies, did dance, and countless musicals. If I had Barbies, I cut off their hair and made them have sex. Once I learned that cleaning gave me praise, my version of playing with toys was lining up all my stuffed animals and admiring them. But, once we went on vacation to Arkansas and saw a cave, and I collected rocks for many years.

To others, my mom bragged that as a kid while riding in the backseat of her car, before I knew cardinal directions or street names, I used to be able to tell her where we were on drives from only seeing the tops of the trees. Maps -- eat your heart out! She'd also brag that I was psychic because once I said, "Aunt C is about to call" and then the phone rang, and it actually was her.

I am, and have always been, a very loud, goofy laugher. My emotional expressions are raw, but for the most part, I never liked to be touched. (It's always been too much, and still is.) Instead, I have many fond memories of time spent in my parent's tub, making as many Avon bubbles as possible, spinning around in circles like a whirlpool, or reenacting both sides of a fictional dramatic scene, sometimes even bringing myself to literal hysterical tears. I remember my mom standing outside the bathroom door a couple times asking me, "Are you okay in there, lil' bird?"

When I was young, I realized my imagination would carry me away, and it had to be my secret. Any part of it that slipped out my mouth, which it often did when I was alone, I had to quiet in other's presence. When I wanted to make noise to myself, I had to immediately stop. My parents would look at me, and I knew they disapproved. They wanted me to be "seen, but not heard".

Other ways, I stood my ground. I asked them "why" and if a reason didn't make sense, I said so.

Like, one time, a new family moved in next door. Their dad was on the Chicago Bears in the 80s. They were an interracial family, and one day, shortly after they moved in, I heard my parents racially gossiping about them in our kitchen. I was just a kid, but I didn't like what I was hearing. It didn't make sense what they were saying. So, I grabbed a double popsicle from our freezer, walked outside, handed the other half to my new neighbor, and introduced myself. We spent a lot of days playing Bomberman 64 in her basement or watching the best of Will Farrell repeatedly.

As a millennial, I was a child in the 90s and 2000s. That means, I was raised on the "Golden Years" of Nickelodeon. As a kid, I could tell you the entire Rugrats episode scene-by-scene from just seeing the very first image of the show pop-up after the title would be displayed. And I did (tell my mom)! I would run over to her, and I would repeat back a scene Angelica was just in, as verbatim as I could, and I was convinced she would be happy. She acted happy for me, and that worked -- for a while. But eventually, I learned she was faking it. But not before (as my mom eventually told as a story) I got in trouble for repeating an Angelica line back to the wrong pre-K teacher during reading time because I was bored, and I told her so, using Angelica's language.

After hearing my mom tell others a few too many stories about me, I learned I couldn't trust her. Throughout my life, I know I projected my early lack of trust at her in ways I didn't understand.

At home, when I wasn't watching the best years of the Sci Fi channel, sitcoms, Nickelodeon, or the same movies (Dancing Princesses, Neverending Story, Princess Bride, The Mask, Snow White [only on Halloween], Beetlejuice, Hocus Pocus, one specific Donald Duck VHS) I was bingeing some of the only foods that I would eat throughout, almost, my entire childhood: cocoa powder, pumpkin seeds, beef jerky/beef stick, French fries, popsicles, fruits (like an entire bag of oranges or something randomly), raw vegetables, and candy (When people weren't looking I'd also sometimes eat weird shit. Like more than a few times I absent-mindedly ate the package the pumpkin seeds came in that were made of plastic and red paint). And, when I say that I ate only these foods, I mean, I *really* ate these things. Like, I ate the **fuck** out of these foods. My boomer parents tried everything that they could to get me to eat other foods, like meat and dairy. Once, they even went so far as to try and force me to sit at the kitchen table for hours, thinking that it would get me to eat canned green beans. Little did they know, the longer those green beans sat out there in the little ceramic dish, they only got colder and less appetizing, strengthening my resolve. Needless to say, I didn't eat those beans, and autonomously chose to go to bed hungry.

If I didn't have food to eat, I always had my nails to bite anyway. And I don't mean in a small way, I mean, when I was young, I would bite my nails so severely that I've made every single finger bleed. And I'd also bite the cuticles around my nails. It was so bad, my mom even bought some of the nail polish that tastes really bad, so you stop. But my lil' bird ass didn't care! I kept biting. Can't stop. I felt like I needed to. But eventually, I stopped. And I do not remember why.

Sometimes I would walk around the house with a pillowcase on the top half of my body with the pillow still inside. It let me lay around the house in my own personal / mobile relaxation station. Other times, I would become obsessed with wearing the same specific renaissance looking dress, walking around the house, or playing video games from morning 'til night, like a forlorn maiden. I went through a phase where I was inspired by the live action movie and video game Tarzan to run around in nothing but underwear, pretending I could swing on vines, and live as a feral child. That was, until I was approaching puberty and my mom sighed, "you're getting too old for this".

The One Time I Almost Died (Because Arby's Had the Meats)

Eventually, in my early single digits my mom took me to the doctor because she wasn't sure if I was going to become malnourished from how little variety I ate. And the doctor told my mom, "If the kid doesn't feel bad, just let them keep doing it". I didn't say I felt bad, so my eating habits continued. After some years, I also ate Arby's roast beefs (or other random, absolutely terrible, meat products. Like at one point during my teens, I would come home and eat paper plate after paper plate of microwaved "grilled" chicken slices). Except, once, I bit into an Arby's beef, and I almost died. I'd be dead if my dad didn't, serendipitously, come out of the shower only to see me choking to death (no coughing, no straw in drink) and save my goofy fucking life.

Honestly, I have never been good at the basic responsibilities of having and upkeeping a human body. I hate brushing my teeth, washing my face, or doing my hair. And, when I was a teen, I was gifted some bottles of peelable face masks and used both of them, basically, every night for -- I don't remember how long. No one saw me do it to tell me to stop. That – mixed with lifelong intense blushing -- destroyed the pores on face from a rather early age. At least in the eyes of the dehumanizing late-stage capitalist commodification culture, claiming we must appear porcelain.

Ironically, in numerous other ways, whenever I noticed "imperfections" on my body, I would immediately remove them. Anything from a mole that was too big on the back of my right arm I scratched off, to pimples during adolescence, attacking mosquito bites with thick bristled brushes until they'd bled and become scarred, and surgically removing ingrown toenails myself. In middle school, if I noticed any peeling skin on the bottom of my feet, I would pick/peel them off. That turned into taking a pair of nail clippers to the thick skin on the bottom of my feet. I would get into a kind of trance. There would be piles and piles of dead skin. It created so many sores I'd have to then bandage up. It would hurt extremely badly to walk that night or sometimes for days. I have distinct memories of having to play softball with wounds on the bottom of my feet from it. I'd have to avoid my urge to limp, like I wasn't in excruciating pain from repeated skin picking.

As a kid, I was gifted a small box TV for Christmas, and spent most of my nights watching Nick at Night until I fell asleep. I'd get so emotionally invested in the plot of "I Love Lucy" episodes that I would have to stop and remind myself that this was not real life and not happening to me.

After I fell asleep, I'd have terrible and incredibly vivid, reoccurring nightmares. Eventually, the only thing that worked was my mom suggesting I sleep next to her mother's rosary. I'd have to hold it in my hand and go under the covers to chase the evil things away that came out at night.

I don't remember how old I was, but once, I remember I woke up in the middle of the night from a nightmare, realizing I'd wet the bed, and told by my mom that I was, "too old to be doing this".

When I was a child, I was called an "old soul" with a "mature humor". In hindsight, this was because of my hyperlexia, stilted speech, and ventriloquizing adults. Yet, as I aged, both my family treated me, and consistently friends left me behind, as if I was "immature" for my age. Whether that was because of how I acted, dressed, or the things I did for fun, it's a clear pattern.

Learning

From an early age, I learned to read beyond my expected grade level. I was the kid in class that would correct the people reading on how to pronounce a word they couldn't – faster than -- or at the same time as -- the teacher. But I learned early that I wasn't "supposed to" be smart. I learned from implicit and explicit observation and interactions that someone seen as a "girl" is not entitled to such things, and people in fact will hate them for that. Around fifth grade, I remember deliberately not trying in school anymore, and made a conscious effort not to appear smart, especially in front of boys. For most of my life, I have earned a completely average 2.6 GPA.

But I learned a lot of this world from living a life of someone who doesn't care about the K-12 education system that existed when I was attending it. While I wasn't dedicating energy towards learning whatever basic information to pass standardized tests and get into AP classes, I spent almost all my energy learning everything I possibly could about human minds and language-use.

On a day-to-day basis, primarily my learning was from just watching people interact. I spent a lot of my early life incredibly confused at what was happening around me, and convincing myself and everyone else around me that I wasn't, while undergoing constant micro-action observations. I thought I was becoming hyper-attuned to what the little motions are supposed to mean. Most of my early life, I was simply watching others exist in a constant backseat mindset of this existence.

My focuses fluctuated with the times. I was raised with the Internet, after all. One of my earliest obsessions was eating disorders. I would spend hours and hours learning everything I could about them on websites where users were reporting their "pro-anorexia" lifestyles in real time. I would beg my mom to drop me off at Borders (when those still existed), so that I could sit in the psychology and self-help sections and learn everything I could get my hands on about anorexia. I became so fixated on it, I started embodying their behaviors myself, until a friend expressed that they were worried about my behavior, and I realized my interest in it was in fact *consuming me*.

That phase continued my already rather complicated relationship with eating. More on this later.

Next, I became intrigued by a related self-harmful path: substance abuse. It started with a phase of reading all of Ellen Hopkin's books about teens, young adults, and adults using hard drugs and repeating abusive cycles of spending, sex, violence, homelessness, and other angsty desperations. After that was wicca. In fact, one time my computer teacher in middle school accused me of burning down a rich family's barn in town just because I had a fucking herbalism book with me.

One day cops showed up at my house and asked if a "[my full name]" lived there. I said "yeah". They asked "ah, is she at home?" and I said "I don't know. I gotta go..."And I went to jump on my neighbor's trampoline, as planned (because ACAB). The bastards followed me there, started questioning me, a whole child without my parents present. They asked, "do you know anything about so-and-so barn?" and my silly kid ass asked back, "Why, did it burn down or something?" Needless to say, they must have really thought I burned the barn down with witchcraft after that. Turned out it was actually just a couple high school kids who didn't put out there cigarettes well.

A lot of my learning occurred through listening to music. I was an emo kid. Around 11, I started with Avril Lavigne and Yellowcard. About 12, I developed a taste for Say Anything, the Used, and Bayside. (So, yes, obviously, I did put the absolute best lyrics into my AIM away messages, thank you!) Unfortunately, their songs frequently romanticized abuse. And, when I get a taste for a certain song, I have a habit of always listening to it on repeat, for days on end. (I still do that.)

There's always been something delicious for me about being in the throe of one particular song.

From a young age, I referred to myself as a lyric's person. I became obsessed with looking them up and knowing exactly what each lyric said. (In hindsight, I could never understand what any of the lyrics said unless I also *saw* the lyrics.) As I would listen, I'd mentally cycle through all the meanings that my brain could muster, referencing my own limited young lifetime. I'd lay in bed, before I went to sleep listening to my favorite CDs, and it'd open a world of memories I'd watch present themselves. I can't invoke images in my head at will. Only in this space, can I see them. (This is the space where my feet do that thing only other autists know about. You know the one.)

It is also the space my poetry comes from. And where my unrequited infatuations are born. It is the secret I have kept closest to my chest. Where all the hyper-fixations of people live on in me. The medium of my frequently one-sided infatuations, and most inappropriate social temptations. I watch bits of phenomena fly around, and catch their slices of life, cutting them into word bits. I chew them in my mouth when reading aloud, real good and gummy, spitting them into your ears.

(This in-between space is also where my three critical media ecological tenants were formed: We only know what we know; Everything becomes normal in repetition; Everything is connected.)

Unfortunately, all my hyper-fixations didn't make me immune from being seen as "the bad guy".

For example, one of the last memories of spending time with my older sister was on a family vacation to a time share in Michigan when I was in my mid-teens. It was the time in my life I had begun to spend almost every car ride only listening to my personal CD player (and burned CDs were finally a thing). So, I would sleep and/or escape into my own mind to watch the memories. On the way to this cabin, I started to notice that the back of my head was getting unusually itchy. This had never happened before, and we were on our way to a vacation, so I kept it to myself thinking it was nothing. I didn't want to be seen as a bother. After hours of driving, we arrived at a couple cabins with a big tree that had a tire swing, overlooking some cove on Lake Michigan.

When we got inside and started to unpack, the itching was spreading and really getting outta hand. I decided to look in the mirror, and what I saw was raised patches, spreading rapidly across more and more of my body, stemming from the back of my neck, head, and ears. When I told my family, they seemed to be rather disappointed that I told them bad news on their vacation. It was almost like they thought I willed a mysterious horrifically itchy break out onto my entire body.

At one point, I remember not knowing what to do, so I sat in the car alone, to not bother them. In efforts to not think about what was unfolding in my body, instead, I repeatedly listened to some burned songs by Dashboard Confessional: Hands Down, Vindicated, As Lovers Go, and Jamie.

Some time passed; now, I was even more miserable. So, my sister suggested that I lay in the sun because maybe that would make the itchy, raised, red bumps go away. Spoiler alert, it Did Not.

A combo of scratching and the sun, my welts *oh so* **Much Worse**. So bad, in fact, they'd spread to the rest of my entire body, including my face. It was funny in a you might die kind of way. My family told me that I looked like the guy from Goonies, kept in the basement. Finally, they began to take my medical woe seriously, and so we left the cabin, and drove to the hospital back home.

These doctors did not know what was going on with me. They just called it an allergic reaction. They recommended I see a skin specialist, and prescribed allergy medications in the meantime.

My torturous welts stayed strong, and too long after that, my mom took me to see said specialist. Realistically, they didn't have many answers, but they recommended I undergo a combination of Zyrtec, Zantec, and ice baths. I remember sitting on the patient table while the doctor told my mom and I that due to the severity of these welts, that if they went internally, I would be dead. Long story short, I spent a number of weeks after that sleeping with ice packs on my face in the wind of many fans, the occasional ice bath, and oscillated between horrific itchiness and numb.

We never found out what I was "allergic" to (if that even ever was the case), besides a couple medications the skin doctor prescribed me to have in attempts to reduce the welts in the first place, making them even worse. This was around 2005, so as luck would have it, it happened to be the time essential oils were arriving on the commodified scene. So, one day, when my parents were away, and my sister was with me, I was inspired to put tea tree on them, and they started fading. Oddly enough, that was the only thing that worked, was covering myself in tea tree oil.

That incident was the single event in my entire life I had ever medically advocated for myself.

I know my family did what they could with the limited knowledge they had, but that entire welt experience perfectly exemplifies the dynamic that constantly played out in our household. When it came to me expressing anything about myself or my needs, it was cast as unserious / made up. Another persistent example of how my family saw me as the bad guy were major U.S. holidays.

Real talk, I hate holidays. And that drove a wedge between my family members and I because they are the days you are unequivocally "supposed to" enjoy. As said, my sister that's eleven years older than me, was always the "good" older child on holidays. She takes part in the entire social charade. Our age gap never allowed us to truly get to know one another. I have both fonder and grimmer memories of when she lived at home. The first grim one that comes to mind, was when she sent me an email telling me the way I dressed was "inappropriate" around adult men in public, including her husband and our own father "because they're only men." (We're polar opposites. I'll expand on how my sister and I's differences collide, within chapter three.)

For me, holidays were always just the days that I was yelled up to (immediately, overstimulated), by my mom, demanding I partake in preparation, and to keep up a social performance of holiday cheer. (The sensitivity I had to a pitch of my mom's voice when she'd yelled up to me "Lil' bird Wake Up; Wake Up Lil' bird!" demanding that I get up early, come downstairs, hangout. That wasn't limited to holidays. Growing up, I was perpetually overstimulated from masking [though, I didn't know that then, this is only something that I'm understanding fully in hindsight] that I would immediately come home and go straight up into my room to decompress from the day.)

(This unknown sensory overstimulation ruined countless days I lived at home with my parents. When it got really bad sometimes as a small child, I would sit inside my own bedroom closet. Once I got older, I would go under all my comforters until I couldn't breathe, and then opened a corner so that fresh air could get in. This is something I sometimes do to this day, when needed.)

Plus, I have never been good at holiday cheer. For most of my life, I'd last until after the meal, and then find – somewhere -- to escape. Anywhere people weren't. Especially, during the hugs goodbye portion. When I was little, I realized I could hide within my mom's side of the closet, under her clothes, and on top of her many shoes that lived inside my parent's bathroom, and I'd lock the door (in fear that they'd make me hug them). As I got older, I realized I was allowed to day drink. That made holidays better -- for at least half of the day. But I still couldn't handle the full day. Years turned to decades until my escaping to my room after dinner became the normal.

On the not holi-days, as soon as I could drive, I was never home. Why…? Well, let me explain.

I'm Not A Family Guy

My parents were both 43 when they had me. Their birthdays were/are a week apart. They were/are boomers. So, I had an old-fashioned childhood compared to most millennials, in that there was lots of good 'ol fashion discriminations of every kind paired with verbal, mental, and emotional abuse that they called "discipline". My parents met through friends at a point in their lives they both never thought they'd date again, yet they immediately connected. They had my sister 11 years earlier than me. So, it should come as no surprise, I was in fact quite a surprise!

My Roma mom grew up in the same working-class town that I lived, drank, and loved in the year before I started my PhD. Growing up she didn't know where her next meal was coming from. When she got married, she was 102 pounds. I know because she'd tell me, conveniently around the same times when she was often reminding me to "suck in my gut" – the years after I'd hit puberty. When you were sick, my mom was the best caretaker you could possibly ask for. She always hosted Thanksgiving and Christmas dinners for all our extended family, and as much as it stressed her out to organize it, she was really good at making sure the traditions were kept alive for our family. She kept the cleanest house I've ever seen in my life (and I've seen a lot of houses, being that we looked for a new one for about fifteen years, but only moved twice in my lifetime). She kept our house as, or even tidier, than most model homes we went to so frequently.

My mom was always a hugger. She always cut up vegetables and put them inside our fridge. Probably because she knew that that was one of the only foods I'd eat as a kid, and that my dad would probably chomp on them too once n' awhile. She always demanded one day we were going to win the lottery. My mom had this habit of telling me what I used to like as a kid, and it always got on my nerves. But I understand now that that was her way of trying to show me that she loved me. She was the biggest Aerosmith fan I'd ever met in my life and drove a dark green Camaro. Her car always wreaked of the sharpest floral perfume. I couldn't stand it. Everything in her car was either too loud or too -- that smell.

Once, when I was a kid, she was delivering Avon in it (as she often did then) and she bought me chicken nuggets for lunch that must have not sat right in my stomach, and I got sick in her backseat -- because the mixture of the car senses, plus motion sickness, must have been too much for my tumtum. One time my mom got really angry, but her face looked funny, and I started laughing and she chased me around the house in rage. My mom couldn't stand it if anything in her house wasn't situated exactly as she wanted it. One time she was yelling at me for putting something in the fridge in the "wrong place", and I asked her what exactly the big deal was about where it was placed, and she only stared blankly at me.

My dad grew up on the same brick road as the first White Castle. He was, allegedly, Irish and raised Catholic as a major part of his identity. I say "allegedly Irish" because our Ancestry.com documentation is shaky, being that his dad (my grandpa) was an orphan. Every day when I still lived at home, my dad absolutely had to eat dinner at 5 pm, or he would get incredibly grumpy. He would salt everything, even pizza. My mom always made jokes about all of that. If we were all out at a restaurant, and he was eavesdropping, the ear on the side he was listening got red, and my mom never let him hear the end of it. She'd tease him about being nosey. My whole life, my dad has had this habit of walking away from the TV during the start of a commercial break and repeating a word or two, over and over, that he'd just heard from whatever he was just watching.

I know little about my dad's early life besides the fact that he loved model trains, he was abused at Catholic schools by nuns who flipped desks and hit you if your shit didn't sit right inside of them, and he was in 'Nam and (like most) it traumatized him. Safe to say, he's seen some shit. His life of actions as a husband and father beforehand show that. My dad is the kind of hard-working boomer guy that was never allowed to feel, or able to express his emotions, until I was in high school. Like, one day my dad had a few Bloody Mary's and became upset about money...

!!! The following passage contains content about a threatened suicide !!!

That night he became convinced my mom and I only loved him for his money, and he proceeded to have a traumatic drunken meltdown, during which he threatened to drive his car into an overpass on the way to work the next day. So, I called the cops, he was then committed for a few days at a hospital. As my dad was being rushed to the hospital nearby, my mom and I drove to meet him in her car, and she said things to me that any child should never have to hear about their own father from their own mother. When we arrived, and he was in intake, he blamed me for calling the cops, saying he was going to lose his job, and that it would be entirely my fault.

My dad's unaliving threat meltdown blaming me was the event that finally got him into therapy, unpacking his repressed emotions and traumas. Years later, he also pulled an Ebenezer Scrooge on us, dying for 15 minutes, and he returned nicer. I've always been more like my dad. My mom said this too when she was alive. I "joke" I got anxiety from my mom and depression from dad.

On average, I don't have tangible memories of my childhood. But if I invite them, some vague memories of how the interactions with my parents went, and what they taught me through them, present themselves. Because of my sister and I's huge age gap, later on, I was raised mostly as if I was an only child.

For instance, my parents expected me to be a lot of things. They expected me to play the piano (my teacher said I could play by ear, but I gave it up because I didn't enjoy it), to be a gymnast, play soccer, and a perfect child that they could mold with discipline. My dad, in particular, made it very clear that I was not allowed to make any mistakes. Because if I did, he spoke and looked at me as if he wished I was never born. Before my older sister was born, they birthed a son, named after my dad. But he lived for an incredibly short time because his lungs were not fully developed (organs that develop late inside utero). While my mom would do her best to impress femininity on me, in other ways, it always seemed like my dad wished I was, instead, born a son. (Technically, both and neither of them were correct in their binary gendered expectations of me.)

My boomer parents never handled arguments in a healthy way, taught me how to cope, or apologized. I remember at a very young age looking down at them from the banister in our first house (where the upstairs looked down upon the living room they spent most of their nights in watching TV) after some sort of extreme emotional or verbal upset between us and trying to judge if they had reached the point yet where they cooled off and pretended it never happened.

In the moments of my childhood when it was only my dad having one of his regular hyper-critical outbursts, in reaction to if I accidentally spilled something, etc., sometimes my mom would swoop in afterward as the "good cop". It was then, she'd remind me -- with conviction --

that I am "so very smart, and not to let anyone –
ever -- let me believe otherwise" about myself.

But then there was the time where something
happened (I don't remember) that upset my mom
enough she said she was going to leave our
family. She drove away saying she'd never come
back. Right after she left, my dad screamed at
me, blaming me that I had pushed my mom to
leave us forever. I don't remember how long
after, but she came back like it had never
happened. I have many memories of running up
to my bedroom, profusely crying, and generally
melting down because of something my parents
said to me that made me feel like I wished I was
never born. The first and only time I ever tried to
kill myself, I was young enough to still have one
of those tiny hand-held kid's pianos in my
bedroom, and I hit myself over the head with it –
hard –repeatedly, wishing I could just die after
one particular argument. I don't even remember
details.

It wasn't easy to take mom's advice. But, I guess,
I should've done what she said, not what she did.
I was raised for most of my life (from 3-years-old
to 24-years-old) inside the big suburban house
my dad's big fancy BP-Amoco job paid for, and
that my creepily older cousin built. My parents
made it clear that where we lived was much
"safer" than about 15 minutes North. We got a
miniature schnauzer, that I named "Rosie," and

she was the best dog in the whole world. Inside
our pantry, we often had tasteless healthy cereal
like grape nuts, shredded wheat, and Special K.

My parents didn't let me "date" until I was
sixteen (I did as much as any millennial did
anyway). My parents did the best that they could
with what they were given, and what they were
almost certainly both given were undiagnosed
autisms, and every discrimination on the market.
For instance, I never truly believed in any
Abrahamic God, but they both did, in some
capacity. I never understood why, and ever since
I was a baby, I rebelled against attending their
churches.

I would cry and cry and cry as an infant, until
they'd give up and drive baby me back home. As
a toddler, more of the same, in itchier more
elaborate outfits they'd put me in to attend hell.
Every Sunday morning felt like some kind of
torture. Time was elusive as a child, and my
tracing the shapes on the outside of the bible
never tided me over for the entire service. I also
hated being made to touch the clammy hands of
strange older people sitting near me. The one
good part of the service was that after third grade,
I got the tasty wafers and wine. (Wine for
children, okay?)

A progressive thing they instilled in me was as
holistic'a sex ed as boomers were able to. And by

"they" I mean mostly my mom. She gave me one of those "everything you need to know about your body, masturbation, and sex" books when I was about 9 years old. I had loads of questions. And while sometimes she was probably annoyed (knowing the voracity of my questioning), as far as I remember, she always offered her honest answers. My mom was diagnosed with lung cancer in 2017 because of poisons brought home on my dad's work clothes. She wasn't allowed to open a bank account in her own name, by herself, until she was in her twenties and took me to the bank as soon as I turned sixteen because -- she'd be **Damned** -- if I didn't have one ASAP.

My mom referred to us as "gypsies", endearingly, her whole life. She taught me to take care of myself financially before anyone else, and certainly not to rely on any man if I can, because of it. Because she lived a life of it. She helped me pay off credit card debt multiple times, and paid for my move to pursue my PhD, shortly after she won her lung cancer blood money. She died at home on hospice in August 2020 because corporations in the United States are allowed to poison our loved ones to death for profit for blood money. I think my mom did the best that she could with what she was given, and what she was given was poison to death. Without my mom, I never would have written my dissertation about sexual ecologies in the algorithmic age or neuroqueer realizations. Because of her, as a kid,

I was the friend you go to for sex questions. Speaking of...

(As I explain much more extensively in chapters four and five, I don't blame my family for only knowing what they knew. This inequitable world and reductive concept of autism failed us all.)

Friends, As Bad As Any Sitcom

Real talk, I don't remember enough to cover my lifetime of friendships. But, I will be taking readers down a path of the more prominent friendships, I do remember, and reflecting on them.

Since I was about four, I played a lot of video games and would ask my dad to go to Hollywood video every Friday to rent a new game. Most days, from morning until night that was how I preferred to spend my focused energy. I was in preschool then, and one of my only memories of being in preschool, besides this, was being chased around by a boy on Halloween day who was dressed as Sonic the Hedgehog. My mom and other parents at the school party told me he must have a crush on me. I learned (young) that boys are predatory if they have feelings for you. It doesn't matter how I actually feel about it. My feelings weren't mentioned to me. I just ran away.

At home, I also played outside. At first it was with little girls who lived across the street. But I realized after a few years that they wanted to play "house," and I was not good at that. My best friend of mine in the neighborhood would come out to play with me nearly every day. When we played outside we would often pretend to be in relationships or made elaborate dances to Disney movie scenes. I had my first kiss with her, while we played Lion King (Simba/Nala) inside of my family' pantry. The two of us also often played video games, or she'd watch me play by myself.

I remember she'd go to "Daddy-Daughter Dances" with her dad, and she made them sound so normal that I asked my parents about them, and they told me I will absolutely *not* be doing that.

We used to play this game in her family's garage where we took these bouncy balls and would whip them out of control at something inside the garage and then apologize to they had hit, and then absolutely die laughing together. Her parents understandably hated it, but that shit was fun. I would have sleepovers at her house, and she told me in the morning silly shit I said in my sleep. Sometimes we'd play Donkey Kong Country 2 or Sunset Riders at her house on Super Nintendo.

One time my family and I visited downtown Chicago, and I had a salad there that included edible flowers. I came home and told her, excitedly, that flowers were edible. And so, we went around that day foraging from our immediate neighbor's flower bushes and eating them. I told my mom when I got home, and she scolded me saying "They could've been poison!" I could've "...needed to get my stomach pumped!" I goofily responded "Well, they weren't, and I didn't ¯_(ツ)_/¯".

A couple of times we hung out in my basement and pretended that some pool balls were our real boobs. We thought it was funny to hold them under our shirts and pretend to act like real adults. My dad caught us doing that once and it was a hilariously embarrassing and ridiculous moment.

Anyway, back to what I was saying about this little neighborhood girl. My first friend. Her older brother always picked on me for reasons I didn't understand. Then, I'd cry and run home. There came a time where the rest of the little girls across the street grew rude to me for reasons I also didn't understand. So, one day, I cussed at one of 'em, and her mom heard, and they ostracized me. Meaning, then on, they always played at the house I wasn't allowed at -- so coincidentally! Not that I'm excusing the fact that I cussed at a neighbor girl who was younger than me. But it did exemplify another point in my life where I simply couldn't get along with other girl children.

Eventually, some other little kids (boys) moved in directly behind my house, and I had much more in common (and fun!) with them, than I ever had with any of my front-of-the-house girl neighbors. We would watch movies, play videos games, or I'd watch the youngest brother play really cool computer games, that I didn't know how to play. They had a ping-pong table, one of those basketball games, a foosball table, a pool table, moon-shoes, and a bunch of other cool toys. They'd have these massive squirt-guns and would invite all the other kids over to fight.

My left next-door neighbors owned authentic restaurants in the area. They had a pool and let neighbor kids swim in it in the Summers, and they hosted family parties many of us attended, regularly. In their pool, we pretended to be mermaids, and I swear I breathed underwater, like magic. I grew up eating their homemade tamales that they'd drop off at our door after making batches. When we were younger, I'd hang out some time with their youngest son, playing Mortal Combat on the hugest TV I'd ever seen in my life at the time. I remember falling once, scraping my knee, and he put a band-aid on it. Then, I realized he was the first person who wasn't my mom to do so. It felt incredibly intimate in a way I didn't know how to feel about at the time. He was always rather flamboyant, and my very first crush was on Elton John -- so -- do the math.

Anyway, I have a vivid memory of being on a very fancy jungle-gym with many boys and them asking me why I don't play with the girls in the neighborhood. I replied, "We don't have much in common. They always want to play 'house' and 'pretend to have babies', and I find that boring". Why would I want to do family stuff, when I could run around and go on adventures and shit....?

As a kid, I remember if I got a drink at one of my friend's houses, I'd notice the smell of the inside of their cups. Like, for some reason, the smell of their house lingered inside there -- the most. I also enjoyed looking inside their families' refrigerators to see what they kept inside it.

As cisheteronormativity would have it, by parents, I was treated like I'd fall in love with one of the backyard boys. He was the middle brother of three. I was not ever in love with him as much as I was taught that he should be a focus of my attention. Pressure makes me incredibly anxious, but I didn't know exactly what my feelings meant at the time. I just knew this is what people told me was supposed to happen, and it made people around me laugh and smile. So, despite feeling more than a bit queasy about the experience, it was kind of fun, in that I didn't know it was fear.

Speaking of kids being mean to me as a child, at some point in grade school I started taking the bus from my house to school. And in doing so, I was bullied so badly that my mom literally paid a neighbor boy to protect me from the bullies there because I would come home crying every day. I don't have recollection of what actually happened there. And that's probably for the best.

This was also around when my mom took me to various daycares, so she could work during the days. The whole place smelled like playdough, and that square cafeteria pizza that's – far -- too oily. My main recollection of that experience is one time she forgot to come pick me up, and I was left waiting with one of the staff members, who tried to be as sympathetic as they could.

Around this age, I remember this one time, I was at a friend's birthday at a bowling alley, and I guess I bit off more than I could chew between chewing gum, drinking a slushie, and devouring pizza, because I went to sneeze and threw up (what looked like the meteor from the start of that one 90s Power Rangers movie) - all over - where the stairs attach to our lane, and cried laughing. In grade school, I had one best friend, and we were both absolutely obsessed, first, with Hanson (which, I promised, was not a phase, and I'd be in love with -- FOREVER), and then, N*SYNC. Most of our in-school friendship revolved around singing N*SYNC songs or pulling out their magazine clippings to admire Justin Timberlake under a waterfall. (If you're a millennial, you know the one.) Shortly after the waterfall centerfold came out, she got a crush on a boy in our class, and I remember feeling pressured to do the same. Like, that was what I was supposed to do. So, I immediately tried to act natural, performing having a crush on that guy's best friend. Because that's what teenagers were doing on the TV. Obviously, a best friend double date was the ultimate idea sold to us, and so regardless of if I was even attracted to boys at all, why not?

I remember that I was also bullied by certain kids at school. The "normal" "pecking order" shit. I have been uncomfortable around people as long as I can remember, stumbling on my words, and I have blushed, profusely on my face and chest (my heart on my sleeve), since I was a kid. The other kids, clearly, picked on the fact I was different, awkward, and they insulted how I looked.

Unfortunately, as soon as middle school came around, N*SYNC friend "developed" early, got an older boyfriend. And, so, apparently, both of these things made her too popular to be with me. If I'm being honest, a lotta my early life I don't remember or couldn't read the room to understand.

As puberty hit and middle school started, I was being bullied more on the bus by other kids, until a neighborhood girl in a more affluent area started to defend me and pulled me under her wing. Her mom owned a car dealership, and she wore mostly Abercrombie and Hollister. (You know the type.) Anyway, her and I became nearly inseparable for a few years. In fact, her mom ended up becoming my God Mother during my confirmation (my dad forced me to take part in "or else I wouldn't be able to live in his house"). For most of that time, I became her naïve follower to survive both on and off the bus. Needless to say, she took full advantage of my vulnerabilities.

My mom would drop me off at her rich mom's house for a day, or sometimes even the entire weekend. Rich friend was skinnier and tanner than me, and it was 2001ish, so peak body-hate. (The 1990s/2000s media industry was absolutely relentless in selling emaciated images of over-sexualized unattainable teenage [typically white or white-washed] AFAB bodies, so every millennial felt even more shame about themselves during one of the most delicate developmental times, making us more vulnerable to commodification. Mind you, I am queer. And I was not allowed to be queer openly for most of my life because I was born and raised in Indiana. I have a vivid memory of being at an afterschool camp one day in elementary school and being called "gay" as an insult by two older kids, while I was doing some pull-ups. Pull-ups are bad enough without homophobia. Luckily, my child mind pulled through. I had no idea what gay meant, yet.)

Anyway, while at this girls' house, I lived on, almost exclusively, one or two honeybuns she'd – sometimes -- let me have. Mind you, no adults ever asked if I ate. That, paired with the fact I was at this person's house (who first protected me from bullies), I felt like it would be too much if I asked for more food to eat. So, denial of regular food for me was treated as apparently normal. (You might be thinking, who's responsibility was it to ensure you ate food? Good question...)

This "friend"'s treatment of me only escalated from there, the longer I was around. She seemed to take pride in treating me like her minion. There were also a couple moments of queerness treated as "our secret," and later lauded over me, "as if I could be so lucky to!". She lived near a neighbor boy that eventually hung out with us sometimes. We were all also on the same school bus. For some reason, I decided to disclose to her that I think I might have a crush on him. She started treating me weird about it when we were alone.

Then, her treatment escalated. One day, he was over and we three went to the side of her house. She started pressuring me to kiss him in front of her. I didn't want to do that. I had never kissed a boy before at the time, and I didn't want my first time to be like that. It made me feel really uncomfortable in a way that I didn't know how to describe. She repeatedly called me "prude" right in front of him for not doing it. It was all really fucking weird. And it was like they were both in on some joke, making fun of me.

One of the last things I remember about our "friendship" was apparently they started seeing each other in whatever capacity. For all I know, maybe they always were, and I was always just some joke to her. Anyway, this last time I remember, she invited me over, and I was treated as a third wheel while her and that same guy started messed around under a blanket. Again, I trusted her and expressed feelings for him. Yet, she treated me as an excuse for her mom, so she wouldn't be "alone" with this guy, rather than a full human with thoughts / feelings that deserved respect.

Luckily, the rest of the friend group that she ate lunch with eventually came to my aid and they all admitted they were concerned for me because she treated me terribly. Long story short, I became nearly inseparable with one of them. At the age of 12, I orphaned myself out at her house almost every weekend to avoid being at home. She lived on the farthest side of town from me, and obviously I couldn't drive yet, so my mom would drop me off and chat with her mom for a while. Stoner friend survived some shit too. We'd walk from her house to the local burger joint, habitually, and split a burger and get some fries. Often, we'd walk to a park down the street; until one night, we went to do that after a bit of drinking, and on the way, I stopped to pee in a bird bath (because peeing in a bird bath as someone who's lifelong nickname is "bird" was a funny thing to do as a tipsy teen), and then an adult man chased us both back to her house. Her mom ended up having to actually get a restraining order against the adult man because afterward he repeatedly walked his dog suspiciously close to her house, and she needed to fucking stop him.

At school lunch time, I'd gravitate around some of the many circles of friends, staying mostly on the periphery of each group. This nice neighbor girl who always tried to be a good person was a swimmer at the time, and I remember trying to do that for a bit too, until I learned I could not physically stand the feeling of wearing a swimming cap and being made to sweat inside water. Her friend group of other swimmers got a lot of homophobic comments thrown at them, and it always made me hurt to see that. But I needed to hide at the time, so I didn't speak up for them.

I have major regrets about not defending them, and sympathy for a deeply closeted version of me.

I remember one time a popular kid pretended to have a crush on me, and I was gullible enough to fall for it. Apparently, he thought I (and my willingness to trust) was a walking / talking "joke".

Seventh grade was also the time when AOL Instant Messenger (AIM) and flip phones arrived. I developed a crush on a boy and asked for an entire class's screennames just to get his. It worked.

We'd chat for hours and hours and hours, late into the night, and I became completely infatuated. Little did I know at the time, we were partaking in a quintessentially millennial secret friendship. I was a deep thinker very young and consumed basic existentialism and psychology, voraciously. I have one distinct memory of hiding Sartre's "No Exit" at Borders so no one else would buy it. Beyond blogging, I reflected on my thoughts within his AIM window all hours of the day/night. In hindsight, it was where a lot of my early interest in identity formation and language bloomed.

Shortly after this was when I started hanging out with punk kids and going to shows (Going to shows let me meet other people who preferred rejecting (or being rejected by) normative society, as well as stimming in public while zonked out in a loud public space with ambiance). This was also the age I started drinking. I held off on weed for year. (Put a pin in this until chapter two.) All my friends smoked but me then, yet one of their mom's accused me of being "the bad guy".

Be *The Bad Guy*

Let's back up, so you can understand how, in other ways, I was, in fact, *the bad guy*. This is a very complicated and nuanced experience that I believe plays out uniquely all over the U.S. Me, I was born and raised in Munster, Indiana, which for anyone who doesn't know, is mostly white. However, they say, the Northwest Indiana "Region" I grew up in is the most socioeconomically and racially diverse area in the country. But, until I was old enough to drive (even just five or ten minutes away from my house, aka for most of my early life), I was mostly living and seeing just exclusively other white people around me. Due to the White Flight, redlining, and gentrification, the school district that I was raised in was one of the richest in the area. Which is to say, at that point in my life (zero until I was sixteen), most everyone that I had ever met had assimilated into United States concepts of whiteness and were speaking the violences of that racial process daily.

Thus, one theme from my early life was seeing and hearing people make comments and alleged "jokes" that were ableist, racist, cisheterosexist, fatphobic, and classist, etc. Except, at the time, I didn't know what any of those things meant. Discriminatory comments were just the words and actions the people around me made as everyday conversation. They were what happened around me, by my family, and those who said they were my friends. People being mean and/or straight up dehumanizing to one another for who they are, was normal. So, in early life, I learned to be "normal" to survive. And I'm not proud of it, but I did my fair share of bullying others for who they were because of how I was treated before that. I learned to be ruthlessly nitpicky towards other kids who struggled socially, at least as much, or more than me. I learned that by doing that, the attention was then taken off of me. A theme as cliché as any 90s Nick' or Disney narratives.

By the time that I entered high school, I had conflicting best friends who I'd spend days with outside of school, and the occasional sleepover. The first, was stoner friend. The second I got connected with through another neighborhood girl (who had moved in later than the boy neighbors) behind my house. As I explained earlier, I'd always had a challenging time making friends with girls, and this neighbor girl was not an exception. But overall, this neighbor girl was/is wholesome and as far as I could tell always made a good effort to be a good person and do the right thing, which I majorly respect her for. However, when we first met, she had been lifelong best friends with another girl, who was not our neighbor. This other girl was sporty thin, very funny, and charismatic. To explain, the town of Munster is divided by a railroad track that separates most newer subdivisions. Due to my dad's BP job, I was raised on the subdivision side, whereas she lived on the other side. Her family is Italian, Cubs fans, obsessed with their shih tzu.

!!! The following passage contains content that includes racial slurs !!!

My most prominent memories of this non-neighbor girl were that, when I was over, we would watch Austin Powers a lot, and then we'd do impressions. I don't remember exactly how it happened, but, eventually, these Austin Powers impressions transitioned into ever-so-casual racist remarks, which she framed as "jokes". Because in the 90s, jokes were often racist as fuck.

She used slurs like "dot heads," "chinks," and "towel heads," that her family clearly taught her, because her dad had absolutely no shame in

saying them himself when people were at his
house.

Racist "jokes" were repeated almost constantly
around me when I was a teenager, as if they were
totally jovial things to say in private. Because
most often when white people in the U.S. say
"we" they often mean "w[e]hite". Because in the
U.S., racisms are historically and factually
"normal".

By struggling to be seen as "normal" as a teen, I
became an enabler of all my friend's bad ideas,
comments, and behaviors. Whether that was
internalized cisheterosexisms, fatphobia, racisms,
or cheating on their boyfriends, and substance
abuse galore. These were all things that not only
hurt myself as a deeply hidden neuroqueer enby,
but also those who were more marginalized than
me.

Which is to say, as a kid who always struggled to fit in, I laughed at and then made those racist jokes back, because the person who said they were my "friend" at the time made them, and I didn't want to get bullied more. Remember, due to color-paved racisms in the United States, as a teenager, the area I was raised in was predominantly white. But it's not like there weren't East or West Asian people around me, just trying to build a life in the U.S without experiencing wide-reaching, taken for granted, and systemic anti-Asian hatred and/or were being pressured to assume a role of an oppressive model minority stereotype. (I didn't know that at the time, or how pervasive they are. Regardless, there's no excuse for my implicit and/or explicit discriminations).

The flip side is her entire Italian family told those racist "jokes" because somewhere along the line, their ancestors assimilated into U.S. concepts of whiteness, and so they did too, losing their culture. There is an exceptionally long history of people newly assimilating into whiteness being racist towards groups of people who have been placed lower on the racial hierarchy than them.

One main inevitability of the race and racialization process of whiteness is it erases and destroys. And I am a product of that cultural destruction myself. I am only this year learning that, being that, I am Roma, and nearly all my ancestors are from somewhere in Czechoslovakia with documentation that does not go back before 1880. Thus, my ancestors were most likely enslaved in Romania for 500 years. For those who don't know, Roma people are still hated internationally. We are stereotypically cast and dehumanized as "gypsies," and "thieves." My ancestors have no homeland to speak of, and I learned that far too late because of their assimilation into whiteness. There is a significant likelihood I will never regain my cultural heritage thanks to their choices.

My point in disclosing this all is that it speaks volumes that these racial slurs and harmful racial stereotyping were taught to me as a kind of "friend bonding" activity. Beyond that (and what I mentioned at the start about my parents' comments on the "safety" of our subdivision), I learned almost all other racisms at an early age from entertainment and news media stereotyping. Again, I knew, maybe, a single Black person in real life then. So, at the impressionable time, that was all I knew. This does not excuse my racisms. It explains how racisms became normal in repetition. And, without a doubt, this is one example among other forms of racial violences I've inflicted.

Some folks, despite seeing who I work to be (twenty-some years later), might understandably react to the racist actions of one of my many past selves and hate me for it. If that person is you, know I understand and respect your reaction. In my own way, that is how I react to the teen stage of myself too. I hope my contextualization of this racism that I was socialized into sparks further reflections for people who, in their unique ways, were taught every discrimination under the sun. Realistically, the internalized fatphobia, classisms, racisms, cisheterosexisms, all run deep in us. I am not a perfect person, I have been molded by this world, like anyone else. Please, understand. It wouldn't be healthy for me to continue to hate a past version of myself that knew what I knew.

(Speaking of things becoming normal in repetition, that "friend" also stopped hanging out with me, entirely, as soon as the opportunity arose to become a popular high school cheerleader. Then, she told me, "…you're so lucky no guy will ever be interested in you just for your looks". A bold claim from someone who conforms to cishet standards, yet I taught how to masturbate.)

Throughout this memoir, I differentiate between my having been 1) *the bad guy* (a) a bad person because I took part in many normalized discriminations, since I either didn't understand, or it was second-nature for me to mimic others around me; b) inability to understand non-autistic flirting because of my life in the sexually violent

U.S. ecology (which inclined me to project resentment onto cismen (those who are assigned male at birth, and then despite gender being made up and changeable, also identify as men), as a group, for violating my body-mind time and time again, and socially perverted my ability to differentiate between where "bullying" ends and "flirting" begins), c) my inability to cope and emotionally regulate (on my own or with others) due to never being taught those skills by my loved ones, which then paired – disastrously -- with my thirty-year-long-unregulated autistic hyper-empathy) and 2) being cast as "the bad guy" aka, being discriminated against for existing as an unrealized autistic person, due to my textbook PDA profile autistic traits: hyperlexia, stilted speech; autistic emotional affect; black and white thinking; my down-played/bastardized social and communication difficulties; my disregard for social hierarchies (that are inequitable and do not make sense); direct speaking style; exhibiting "non-feminine enough" characteristics; overly literal autistic interpretation patterns; compulsory heterosexuality as a repressed queer millennial, etc. It is crucial to mention, I was discriminated against for being textbook autistic, before knowing I was and before traumas. In certain regards, my autism made me significantly more vulnerable to abuse and sexual violences. In other ways, as you will see in chapter two, my autistic ability to mask while falsely imprisoned protected me.

(From ableist eyes, my autism systematically excludes me from my humanity, and delegitimates my research expertise. Ableists, inside and outside of academia are notorious for ventriloquizing ahistorical, eugenicist, and fascist rhetorics, that have been built into this system as features. For this, and more, my main message is how humans act *as* media in our society building processes.)

In an unlikely turn of events, one early lesson, that grounds the motivation for my critical media ecological work, stems from my first job at the BK Lounge (Burger King). I could not drive on my own yet, but I had my drivers permit, so I was Damn Close. Shortly after I got the job, my parents surprised me by showing up to my job in a white soft top cavalier convertible. Honestly, it was one of the coolest things they ever did for me, besides give birth. I was very lucky to have it, and I had many nice drives in that little car. That job was an okay first job, in that, it wasn't all that difficult even though it majorly stressed me out, and I absolutely snuck and ate – far -- over my wages in slushies, grilled chickens, and chicken fries with my co-workers. I really loved my coworkers at that job, most of them were very cool, and much different people than I'd ever met before, in that, they were from nearby towns in areas I hadn't yet spent time in, at the age of 16. (I expand on a few more influential lessons I learned from coworkers there within chapter two.)

!!! The following passage contains content about suicide !!!

Tragically, not too long into this job, one of my teen coworkers killed himself. It was shocking. Our high school was devastated by it. Nothing like that had ever happened during my time there.

I didn't know him that well, but I'd worked plenty of shifts with the guy and he was one of the funniest and seemingly most happy guys I'd ever met. (But isn't that what people almost always say after?) A lot more people seemed to love him than he knew. His funeral line seemed endless. (Not that you can always judge if people genuinely cared by if they attend someone's funeral.) It made me realize that even someone who appeared so loved could feel completely alone anyway. Did he feel like he was the bad guy too? If I can, I want to make sure no one ever feels like that.

This is also why I am sharing my life from a Dr. bird's eye view. Both as an expert of identities, language, intimacies, and institutions, and a millennial who's made life-changing neuroqueer self-realizations. My hope in writing this, is that my doing so will reveal how I was introduced to discriminations, worked to unlearn them, while enduring unique ableisms and cisheterosexisms.

Throughout my life, I have both contributed to racisms and been oppressed in many other ways (most of which, as they happened, because of my unrecognized autism, I didn't understand then). That's the violent challenge of being born into world where multiple forms of oppression bleed into each other, simultaneously. My experience as an unrealized autist inclined me to trust others to do the right thing and I then mimic or repeat them without being able to know, or possibly grasp, the fullness of historically oppressive structures as a child. This is exactly how oppressive language usage frequently works, inevitably leading us to hurt ourselves and others in confusion.

Again, my experience could never, and does not, represent all autists. And I would never claim that they do. But, in a world built as inequitably as this one, in my early life, I was complicit and discriminatory. We were all born into a world that existed long before we got here and live the violences of that. I believe there is a strength to be gained from acknowledging both the ways that we are raised into committing acts of violence, as well as telling tales of surviving violences.

Inevitably, most all of us alive today are situated in both positions of benefitting as some type of oppressor, and in other ways, experiencing oppression. I am of the opinion that oppressors [past and present] should be more open about how they harm, as a part of dismantling / decolonizing.

This book transparently documents my unrealized, substance abusing, sexually violated autism.

As you will see, most of my life, I wasn't myself at all. It was much easier to live as *the bad guy*.

In a world as inequitable as this one, by most, I have been welcomed, praised, and embraced for staying silent in the face of discriminations, and thus, was matter-of-factly being *the bad guy*. I was the bad person that people preferred. Now, ever since my twenties, due to taken for granted discrimination against autists, my sharing knowledge / direct speaking make me "the bad guy".

Chapter Two. Requirement Politics? Full-Time Drinker

Allow me to lift up the metaphorical pin that I stuck in the previous chapter, where I mentioned I started drinking when I was about 12 years old. Then, drinking was just something to do for fun.

I remember the very first time that I went to stand up after drinking a little too much and feeling that weight in my legs where you begin to lose complete and total sober control of them. Stoner friend joked that not everyone becomes an alcoholic just because they drink as young as we did. The strangest part is, with what I know now, I'm not even sure if I can claim it. Let me explain...

Sense-Making

Since I was a toddler, I have always had an oral fixation. Hence my persistent, ultimately self-harmful, and all-around bad, childhood habit of nail biting. As I grew older, the way I have met that need was through eating, chewing the inside of my cheeks, and lips, or as I grew, drinking and sex. Drinking wasn't always necessarily alcoholic. In fact, I have never really enjoyed home alone alcohol. It's something I have around others. And being that alcohol is a U.S. social staple. Well, you do the math. When I am out in a social function, my natural inclination is to drink. It was the one main thing to do with my hands, that everyone else was doing, acting like an anchor. The thing about leaning on alcohol to stabilize you is: if you drink too much, it will fucking kill you. Hence why, the most miraculous part of my writing my own memoir is: I am alive to do so.

I have a piece coming out in Art/Research International journal called "Requirement Politics" in which I describe the sexually violent U.S. ecology. In this memoir, I have decided not to include any specific details about my being preyed on by Internet pedophiles. No one is entitled to that. But what I will say is that as a millennial, raised with the Internet, I had my America Online (AOL) screenname by 7. And pedophiles, of all genders, preyed on our generation. I was no exception to that. And, unfortunately, you have no idea who anyone is behind their keyboards.

Between my oral fixation and my expressive nature; I am a very sexual person. From a young age, I was raised not to be sexually ashamed. And when I was younger, I remember feeling in my element sexually. However, as I disclosed more extensively in "Requirement Politics," besides the pedophiles, like many millennials, I was also exposed to violent porn very young. I had seen just about everything the early Internet had to offer -- by my teens. I remember thinking pornstars who were older than 21 were retiring age. In a sense, was my young mind wrong? No. Twenty years later, it's just an absolutely terrifying and absurd observation that a young me had.

I will not detail my sexuality in my early life, but I will say I'm a fan of Big Mouth and Pen15. I was a very thin kid and have memories of being flat chested and trying to make boobs manifest. Not because I actually feel right with having breasts, but because that is what society demanded. At this age, I was possessed with cishet. propaganda about wearing a bra and shaving my legs. It became my main prerogative to meet the stereotypical milestones of my friends, doing the same.

In recent years, I have often thought about how in this lifetime alone, I can say -- with absolute certainty -- that more orgasms have happened than any previous lifetimes in human history, due to reformisms, increased comprehensive sex education, and affordable advanced sex tech. And by myself, I have had an infinitely more fulfilling sex life than I ever had with any cisman to date. (This should come as no surprise, literally and figuratively since I wrote my diss. on it.)

For real though, for most of human history, violent sex was the man-made order. It still is, and remains, mostly uncriminalized. Alongside the violence, some people with vulvas can now also have orgasms. Not all, but more than ever before in history. Quite literally, almost parallel to the massive ongoing doubling in knowledge, one person with a vulva within this lifetime could have more orgasms now than the rest of people with vulvas for most of human history. This is why in my dissertation I called the orgasm gap what it is: the cisheteronormative orgasm gap. It is an orgasm gap that resulted from the devaluation, exploitation, and violence inflicted on folks with vulvas. The way we describe the orgasm gap is of the utmost importance, as well as not calling the vulva the "vagina". As many others have been more vocal about in recent years, calling the vulva "the vagina" erases the clitoris. The language we use has tangible impact on pleasure. And since you cannot talk about sex without talking about violence, language usage also inclines violence. (Unfortunately, when I was in my teens and twenties, I did not know any of this yet.)

This is all to say that despite the fact I was raised to be an autonomous sexual person, most of my experiences of sex with cismen from late teens until late twenties were still exceptionally violent. I know what I like and how I like it, but I was no match for gendered and autistic stereotypes of following cismen's lead. And in this society, my following their lead meant I don't orgasm. It meant, my role is to pretend to enjoy the experience, be incredibly generous, and they finish. If sex with cismen (at the time) taught me anything, it's that my body and mind don't matter at all. So, even if I ended up having sex with one of them, I became uncomfortable with being myself.

Why wouldn't I? It was made abundantly clear to me, ASAP, that I was not safe around them. If it wasn't from the persistently discriminatory comments about key aspects of my being that they made as "jokes" in public, it was pervasive sexual harassment and repeated sexual violence. I very much wanted to have sex with cismen that was fulfilling, I just couldn't because of them.

To be clear, I do not consider every single time I had sex after drinking alcohol sexual violence. Sometimes after, I consented and kind of enjoyed the experience. Other times, I was blackout drunk, and since no one can consent to being sexual with anyone blackout, definitively, I was r***d. Thus, like 9 out of 10 autistic AFAB folks, I've survived lifelong sexual violence. As not to repeat myself here and in "Requirement Politics",

I will only share details I didn't there. I will not be including every sexual violence I've survived, but for a fuller picture, read that piece too.

Smells like Teenage Spirits

At the start of middle school, I think without knowing it, I was embodying iconic androgyny. Large t-shirt, barely any pants. I barely considered how I looked. By 7th grade, that changed. The pressure hit, and I conformed, badly. This was around the time I got my first period, and I think it changed my self-perception. I don't know if it was because my mom treated me getting my period as a special "girl" thing, or what. She made sure I knew that I should get chocolate and be treated better on my period. Anyway, I started brushing my hair more and trying to look femme. I remember putting on lip gloss in the same bathroom where kids got in trouble for putting each other out in sleeper holds, when that was a trend. (Yes, we did ridiculous shit before TikTok.)

Somehow, around this age, my parents won the little lotto, and we took stoner friend on a cruise. It was funny because one stop was Jamaica, and we could drink on the excursion in public. But when we entered, and I ended up winning a booty shaking contest, I was too young to get the congratulatory shot they'd pour into winner's mouths. So, make that make sense, for a second. I was young enough to shake my ass, but too young to drink in accordance with the contest rules? It was ass backwards, literally and figuratively. I have such a visceral memory of us getting back to the ship afterward, with our foot-tall alcoholic margheritas, running up twelve flights of stairs.

Strangely enough, we went only three months before Hurricane Katrina hit New Orleans (where our port was). By far the most fucked up part about that cruise though is that we made friends with some other teens our age, and then one night I heard rumors that some of them had an orgy that someone (undisclosed age?) recorded it all on the top deck of the ship one night. We were only 15 at the time, but I remember stoner friend and I pointed out that that was child porn and fucked up. Really, my brain couldn't yet compute that it was a sex crime I should have reported.

In my teens and twenties, I drank because it was fun and cool. I also drank because it allowed me to let loose and hang out with friends. Drinking was always *So Fun*, until it Very Much *Was **Not***. The first time I ever got black out drunk, I was 12 years old. My stoner friend and I walked a couple of blocks to a house having a bonfire. I have no recollection of what happened. I don't remember when I started drinking that night. All I have left are a few vague mental snapshots, like polaroids of the night: the bonfire, someone lying that someone else ate something they were allergic to (to the mom who's house we were all at), and then I woke up the next morning on my stoner friend's couch. Two kids carried me home. They all made fun of me for how I was when I blacked out. I went home and told my mom. She was a really good sport about it. She asked me "Do you feel like shit?" I said "yeah" she replied "Then don't do it again! You're not in trouble."

My stoner friend and I did have a lot of fun together during middle school. She really was one of the best friends I ever had. Her and her other friends were doing Xanax bars and all other kinds of harder shit, that I never did. I don't know how I didn't, to be honest. I have a very addictive personality, but something always stopped me from doing anything more than booze/weed at any age. I knew I feel A LOT -- at baseline. We'd walk all around town and hang out at the skatepark with skater boys. The first time I ever kissed a boy, I was playing spin the bottle with them inside a blow-up bouncy castle. (Too many of them also grew up far too early. I'd read their memoirs.)

In middle school, I started learning French, but could never grasp lessons of future pejorative, so I gave up, despite continuing on to take advanced classes until my junior year of high school. (I guess you could say that I'm a much bigger fan of French kissing than of the language itself. This was why I was able to hide that French copy of Sartre's "No Exit" I hid to return to, often.)

This was when I learned that my friends went to a school therapist because family trauma, yet I thought that my family wasn't abusive. Like, I have a distinct memory of feeling bad that they had such a hard early life in their families, as if I did not in fact also live a childhood that was full of emotional, verbal, and mental abuse (too amidst everything, being normal in repetition).

As time passed, and often happened, stoner friend and another girl got closer, and they both left me behind for reasons I don't think I'll ever fully understand. If memory serves, we split ways for a couple reasons. First, because her and that other conflicting best friend (the same one who made racist "jokes") shamed them for weed. And then, also, because her and our newer ballerina friend bonded over both having older boyfriends, getting birth control shots, and pursuing the grueling process of selling their eggs to strangers for thousands of dollars. I couldn't understand.

(If I haven't already made it clear, that is the consistent pattern of many of my early friendships.)

High and Low School

Meanwhile, my goofy fuckin ass was wearing my crew uniform at the BK Lounge. But getting to know my coworkers also made me much more aware of many social problems. Like, cops racial profiling folks, and the way that sometimes you have to hide a gun inside the air vent of your car to protect yourself. That, no matter how innocent Black folks are, they continue to be pulled over for being Black. From working the morning shift, I also learned that Burger King was cutting the hours of an elderly women who needed to pay medical bills, to put me on shift instead because I was a younger, faster worker. It gave me a lot of perspective on how the workforce *really* works.

Eventually from being there so much, I got a crush on one of my coworkers. He was my age and from a couple towns over. One day he invited me to a house party at his friend's. He couldn't drive, so that night, I picked him up and we drove there. Once we got inside, I realized what kind of place it was. This was not the first trap house I'd been to and walking downstairs confirmed it. There were a bunch of people downstairs hanging out, and a card table with a bunch of drugs. It was like walking into a candy shop for drug addicts, in that, instead of candy, it was *just drugs*.

By this age, I already knew not to act like this was a big deal. This was totally "normal", and I was *absolutely fine* with what was happening around me. This boy was my crush. This was his friend's house, so I can't "disrespect the hosts". That would be *rude*. Where **are** my *manners*...?

Anyway, that night we made out a whole bunch, and I got the highest (just weed) I'd ever been in my life, at that age. We slept on a pull-out couch, and by the time we were laying down for bed, I was so high, that I couldn't tell what words were coming out of my mouth, and which were my thoughts. He got handsy with me, but I have no real recollection. That night was the first time I was ever scared, the day after, what might've happened to me, since I was fucked up.

That fling with him didn't last past that night, and that's perfectly fine with me because of that.

While working there was also the one time in my life that I was regularly getting my nails done at salons, even though all that ever happened is the meat juice and mayo would get stuck under 'em. I honestly couldn't have imagined a worse time for me to have gotten expensive fake nails. (But they did allow me to stim more openly in public in a way that I did enjoy and kept a secret.)

The one thing I persistently hung onto in my life was that one AIM guy from seven grade. When we were younger, he introduced me to online poker, before it became illegal to play for cash. But when I'd see him in school, or around his friends, he would act like we didn't talk as often as we did. He was always really goofy, observant, vulgar, suspicious. Like, his sense of humor was always a cross between Mr. Bean and Tim and Eric. We mostly had rather similar music tastes.

The thing about those millennial online friendships: they were often hidden for a reason. And as much as I appreciated our frequent exchanges, being that talking with him served as a place where we hashed out a lot of things, most of the time he was sending me mixed sexual messages that he was interested in me, and then, later on, he'd treat me, as if he never said them. (But, who knows, maybe I just truly don't understand *ANY* social cues *at all*, and I misunderstood him...?)

Speaking of bullshit, I moved on up to mall jobs, just far enough away for pay not to be worth it. My first mall retail job was working Christmas season at American Eagle. My skills of folding shit really came in handy. I made the jeans and sweaters look 😗 👌 for all of five seconds before countless strangers came in, messing up my hard work to: pick 'em up, unfold them briefly, and, almost immediately, set them down, for me to refold again. If that wasn't bad enough, I had to pedal the most bullshit corporate slogans like "Sweaters are buy one get one half off" and shit. Easily one of the most eye-opening experiences of the job though was when one night we were stocking the store back up and one of my coworkers asked me "if I don't believe in God..." why I "...don't just go around murdering people?" They dead ass asked me this inside American Eagle.

Safe to say, I got out of that job, and then briefly worked at dELiA*s which, honestly, was awful. The folding felt somehow worse, the emotional labor was exceptional because it was mostly teen girls who had been made to feel incredibly self-conscious about their entire bodies since birth. 0/10; I would never work in a store like that again. It was girl bossing before girl bossing existed.

I attended both my junior year and senior year proms. Neither were worth it to me. Junior year, I attended as a double date with my stoner friend and this guy she was dating and his best friend. They showed up to my house for pictures stoned out of their fucking minds. I don't remember the rest of the entire night. (If readers haven't noticed, I do not often care for social traditions.)

Senior year, I went with my boyfriend at the time who was quite the eclectic fella. In hindsight, he was almost certainly also autistic (but only he knows). He wasn't my usual type, if I'm being perfectly honest. Not that I had a type besides maybe like goofy weirdo. Anyway, I dated him for a remarkably short time. I gave him his first kiss, and immediately after, I pat him on the head. I didn't mean to be patronizing about it, but honestly, I didn't know what else to do after that, and I frequently have awful (yet in the future, rather) comedic timing. This guy was from the next town over, acted in a school play, was obsessed with the song Flagpole Sitter by Harvey Danger, and him and some of his friends introduced me to the cult classic, Rocky Horror Picture Show.

I mean no disrespect by saying this, but the longer I dated this guy, the more all I could see was Frankenstein's monster. So, we only kissed a few times, but I liked hanging out with his friends.

Eventually, after a much longer coupling than should've gone on, I broke up with him, and then I hung out with his friends for many years afterwards. This new friend group was a rather rag tag group of people I am certain I would have otherwise never gotten to know. They were a mix of working-class people who loved guns, hunting, and pretending to go out with their CV radios on a patrol (and sometime ghost hunts that I never took part in because I am just a scaredy lil' bird).

This group looked down on weed, but occasionally, they had parties where we'd drink a bit. They were a welcome reprieve, that felt rather innocent and wholesome in comparison to my usual. They were as obsessed with horror movies as I was, but also watched far too many action movies for my liking. But I watched those with them too and fell asleep. In fact, it warms my heart how many nights the closest friend and his family let me eat at their house and sleep on their downstairs couches. I can never repay them for that, and it meant everything to me. I was the first person he ever told that he was queer and had a secret relationship with someone in California. He certainly thought he couldn't tell his parents, and I understood that, completely.

His California boo-thing eventually came to visit, and I met them. But the vibe was off, so they cut ties not too long after that. His dad was also a member of a Veterans Club / mostly a bar to buy raffle tickets in East Chicago. And when we were old enough to legally drink, we would often go there and hangout with all the older men and drink cheaply. At one point, we made a pact that if we didn't get married by the age of thirty, we'd get married, but he is a cop now (and, honestly, that is no surprise because of what he believed then about cops, and that entire group's patrol tendencies, even though the carceral system was created to reinforce white supremacy, and he is

Latino. Not that there aren't many Latino people these days reinforcing white supremacy).

As high school came to a close, my parents insisted I have a high school graduation party. Close by family members, neighbors, and friends were invited, and there was a bouncy castle, catering, and all the bells and whistles. But whether because of bad scheduling, or my inability to socially connect with people from my actual high school, no kids showed up who RSVP'd, except for a single girl (who tried to be nice and jump in the bounce castle with me, and then left after). That was absolutely devastating and embarrassing, but most of the time I forget that it even happened.

That One Time I Attended Chaos Colleges

Sooner or later, I learned that AIM friend was betraying my trust. In that, without my knowledge, sometimes his friends would be chatting with me on his account. His friends treated me as some kind of naïve sexualized joke that they could take advantage of behind a keyboard. And, later, to my face. Like, for instance, I have a memory years later when I was home visiting from college.

The racist "joke" high school friend and I went in his friend's hot tub. In hindsight, if what I later realized might have happened, in fact, happened, he'd committed a "revenge porn" crime. I say that, having good reasons to believe it wouldn't have been his first offense in the state of Indiana. That was just one example, after years, of all of those people taking advantage of my naivety, each in their own way. Because racist "joke" old "friend" often put me down in front of them.

In fact, after she went away to college, she became a total stoner. Hella hypocritical, since (if you remember what I said) she used to talk shit about that other stoner best friend of mine for that. Anyway, smoking weed was all she wanted to do when she came back to town. After seeing her a couple times, and her belittling me some more in front of those guys, I finally stood up to her. Ironically, I ended our "friendship" in front of hot tub guy's house, for never being a good friend.

Speaking of college, my first year I went to Ball State for social work because that's what my sister did, and I was always the therapist friend. I knew I wanted to help people, but I didn't know how. That first year of college was a wake-up call. I was on my own for the first time in my life in the most depressing place on earth: Muncie, Indiana. The college campus is great, but the rest of the town -- fucking blows -- especially when you don't have a car nearby to escape it. This was the first and last time in my life, so far, that I started taking anti-depressants. The ones I was on made me unable to physically cry until six-months after I stopped taking them. I cold turkeyed (not taking) them, experiencing some of those brain zaps pill bottles warn you about.

Most of that year I spent freaking the fuck out, or inside one guy's dorm room. He was a bigger guy with a cleft palate he was self-conscious about, who disclosed to me he did everything he could to blend in with the crowd. Despite a conformist life philosophy, this guy had surprisingly great taste in music, introducing me to bands like Of Montreal and MGMT. We had a lot of fun for about a year. It made me realize I was not going to be able to emotionally handle social work, and I went to therapy for the first time since after my dad's major unalive threat meltdown. That therapist added "anxiety" to my diagnosis of "depression". (Quite the notorious duo those too!) Anyway, I needed to get the fuck out of there, so that guy and I attempted to transfer elsewhere. It didn't work, so I ended up taking a semester off of college, moving back home with my parents again, and trying, but failing, to get a serious adult job with only a high school diploma.

The year was 2009, and so I could not find what did not fucking exist. But what I did find, instead of a good job with only a diploma, was an older boyfriend from the next town over who looked like Chad Michael Murray. Long story short, this guy was a total misogynist. And what I mean by that is, is that he would treat us like we were an elderly couple in an outdated sitcom.

I stayed because, at first, we had sex in my car and outside. It was never very good sex, but it sure was exciting! Other than that, this one time we went to a strip mall pet store and a miniature schnauzer was there. My first dog, Rosie (who we had since I was 4) had passed away only a few years prior to this time. It hit me really hard because I know she suffered a lot near the end of her life. She died at home on July 3rd, while I was out at the town fireworks show with some friends.

Anyway, I played with this mini schnauzer in one of those play areas, and I absolutely lost it. I was bawling my fucking eyes out, and I knew I needed to save this dog from this pet shop. She looked just like a baby Rosie. So, I impulsively bought her with a credit card. But I was 19 years old and had no idea how to train a dog. I was living with my parents, so the only place she could live was my bedroom. I was completely in over my head from my impulsivity, and so later my mom found a better home for her because I was unable to give her the full care that she deserved. Goddess knows, I couldn't even care for myself. I was in no position to be a full-time dog parent.

Back to Chad Michael Misogynist. The longer we dated, I barely ever wanted to have sex with him anymore for reasons that made me uncomfortable to think about. He took it personally. On one hand, I can't blame him because he is a human that has needs. However, one night he was over at my parent's house, and we were having a bonfire, which was very unusual for us. As far as I remember, that was the first and last time a bonfire ever happened at that first house (and this was the house I spent my life in from the ages of 3-24). Anyway, I was on my period at the time, and I got really drunk because the entire situation probably made me very uncomfortable. He was drinking as well, but he didn't get anywhere near as drunk as I had. Plan was that he would sleep across the hall in the spare bedroom, and I'd sleep alone in my childhood bedroom. I don't remember what happened besides a single memory of lying in my childhood bed and he was on top of me. I absolutely had not consented to sex. Then, I forgot about that night until much later. Because for those of you have not experienced being raped, or heavy drinking, that is common.

***

Some period of time went on, and I began to notice that something Very Off was going on with my, ya know. I couldn't explain it, but something Did *Not* Feel Right. I knew I needed to see a gynecologist. But I was like 19, so I did what any teenager does and went to Planned Parenthood.

Next thing I knew, I had my feet up in stirrups, and a doctor lady was prying what looked like a smashed strawberry out from my insides. Surprise -- that night that C. M. Misogynist r'ed me, I actually had a tampon still in! Because I was on my period, drunk, and never consented to sex.

The gynecologist asked me if I wanted to "tell her anything", and I didn't know what to say to her. I just got up and left in utter and complete shock. Not just from the Toxic Shock Syndrome that surely should have killed me (from having that used tampon rotting up inside of me for -- who knows how long!!!). Mind you, I was still with C. M. M****r at the time. We certainly had no sex. I told him what I learned, and he didn't have much to say. Last thing I remember about our "relationship" was that he cheated on me at his best friend's birthday party after I'd left. His birthday and Valentine's Day were a few days apart, and he had the absolute nerve to tell me he cheated on me in a Best Buy (where he worked) parking lot and after I'd given him $200 in gifts.

If I'm being perfectly honest, I don't have any recollection of how I became friends with the person I went to -- immediately after C. M. Mush told me he cheated on me, and I lost hundreds. But I was a fucking wreck. Mostly, probably, because my body was carrying the trauma of now not only having been r***ed by someone who claimed to "love me," but also being cheated on too. As it goes, I hung out with this friend and frequented their group for a while post-breakup. Her musical influences on me: Star Fucking Hipsters, Modest Mouse, Kimya Dawson, Peaches.

Anyway, we'd drink, smoke, and have bonfires. There was lots of Led Zeppelin and the Grateful Dead playing at those bonfires. The group was a welcome change from dating someone, who, in hindsight, I didn't enjoy being around, and then they r****d and cheated on me. Every once in a while, we'd call Church of Scientology and ask to speak to Lord Xenu. Until one day they knew one of our names, and so we stopped calling, since we had better things to do than be murdered.

Shortly after this, I decided to return to college because, I could not find a real job, and I needed some kind of direction in my life. I arrived at the Purdue Calumet office of registration and records. I asked for the list of degrees, closed my eyes, and dropped a finger on Sociology. This began my six-and-half-year part-time (in hindsight self-accommodated) bachelor's degree life. I started out very disappointed that I was back in the area at the one university I always said I wouldn't attend. People in the town I grew up in looked down on Purdue Cal because it's always been more of a community college that began to market itself more as a "destination campus". (There is nothing lesser about colleges of any kind, and it was arrogant of me to ever think that.)

One summer day the post-break up friend asked if I could drive them somewhere because they were going to adopt a kitten. I'm allergic to cats, but I decided to go with them because that was my friendly duties. We arrived to find a bunch of cute kittens inside of a baby bassinet, and she asked me "which one do you think I should get?" and I responded, "I don't know, but this one's mine!" That kitten was Twinkle. It took a few weeks before she was old enough to come home with me, but eventually she did. I wasn't allergic to her as a kitten, and she slept in my bed with me, even though she was so very small. I was still living with my parents at the time, and so she spent almost all of her earliest life inside my bedroom, being a tiny menace to the cause, only because at the time, my parents both did not want a cat (my mom was allergic too, and dad just never thought he liked cats) because they had recently adopted a huge Doberman named Naomi.

Naomi was the goofiest fucking dog we ever had. I joked she had the name of a stripper (all love to sex workers and stay tuned for more on sex work, later in this chapter) and she had the most overt personality I had ever seen in a dog. Maybe it was just her large size, but she really felt personified to me (even in comparison to Rosie). I have one particular memory of my dad yelling at Naomi and blaming her for throwing up, threatening, and raising his hand to hit her. I ran to her defense – so fast -- yelling at him "not to dare talk to her like that or raise a fucking hand to her ever again". I'd never done that before. Right afterward, I took her outside onto our deck and sat with her on the stairs, trying to calm her down, and sobbed my fucking eyes out, holding her.

Post-break up friend grew up with an abusive father. And she really needed to leave his house. So, I decided to try to help her do that with student loans, I got, starting up college again (even though I knew she did not have a job at that time). In an ***unforeseeable turn of events***, this – completely -- backfired on me. Not only did I still have that new miniature schnauzer that I could not take care of on my own, but I also learned she was not treating "finding a new job" seriously. The little loans I had coming, could not support us both forever. I think we had that apartment for maybe a little over a month. Long enough to have a few drunken nights where you pour a whole container of purple Kool-Aid into a handle of Smirnoff Vodka and play drinking games. We all laughed and cried about our different and shared traumas. Turns out the place had bed bugs. I found out because I got little bites on my ankles, and pupper was straight up having a bad time.

And, honestly, it was for the best. Because I sure as fuck couldn't afford to support us anymore. Debt friend ended up owning me about $700 afterward, that she tried her best to pay back. But it, ultimately, drove too big of wedge between us. Well, that, and this other time that we drove to an apartment in the town my dad grew up in, and we arrived, and I saw heroine for the first time. To be honest, when I saw it, I thought it was cocaine. Those white powder drugs are too confusing! But seriously, I knew I needed to get the fuck out of dodge - as soon as I saw that. No, thank you.

(Obviously, all love to anyone who has struggled with hard drug addiction. All I mean is that, as soon as I learned that it was heroine, I knew I was too close. And I have an addictive personality. It was a mixture of both concern for this friend, as well as upset she'd bring me around heroine.)

The Traumatizing Twenties

At some point during 2010, my parents decided that I should move into an apartment because we simply could not coexist whenever I lived at home. My dad agreed to pay for my apartment lease in the next town. Most of the time that I stayed there, I could barely afford food or wasn't home.

Speaking of things that are bad for you, all jokes aside, I've been a horror fan my entire life. One of my major scripts is that "throughout my life, I have probably seen more horror films than most people have seen films in general". (It really says something about a person if they willingly watch horror movies to relax. Looking at myself.) For this reason, alongside needing a little bit of money, when I was 20, I decided to apply to work a season at the Spirit Halloween store.

From doing so, I learned that Halloween stores keep their shit in warehouses all year, and pay employees dirt cheap to build a store inside other, usually, previously foreclosed stores (Circuit

Cities, Mattress Stores, etc.), using only cork board and zip ties. Their company boards must have just decided it wasn't worth the profit for the already bare minimum cost. Their business plan is a major rip off that makes everything in the vicinity wreak of putrid rubber. In 2010, that thing stinking like a plastic storage tub was me. (Man, I swear that old Circuit City was haunted.)

You know how spiritualists will say that people who eventually meet circulate around each other until, serendipitously, they finally smack faces? Well, one unexplainable memory I have while working at Spirit was exactly like that. A person I spent far too much time with after the age of 21 somehow came into the store with his jocky/nerdy friends and came up to me while I was working there. They were all raised into the same Lutheran school as the neighborhood girl I had my first kiss with. They approached me, asked some fake goofy questions that teetered between mocking me and flirting with me, and put some nearby masks on. It was an absolute fever dream.

Working at Spencer's Gifts the year after their Halloween store, realistically wasn't much better than being possessed by an actual demon. I folded lots of sexist ass shirts. I was there during the era of those rubber wrist bands. And kids stole them by the dozen. They would arrive in packs and hoard around the baskets of those bands. We never stood a chance. Other customers came in and made the same jokes about the Great American Challenge (google it). Then there were the packs of juggalos with one juggalette in parachute pants. On the bright side, I got dibs on jewelry at a discount for the many piercings I got. It was the year of Tiger Blood and flatbacks. At work, I put away and organized a lot of shot glasses, lingerie, and cleaned up some broken lava lamps. The worst thing that happened was, one time a real adult man called the store, breathing heavy, and asked me to "set the phone down, so he could hear the store sounds, and let him finish".

Around this time, I met a communist guy who would drive me and his friend around, and we'd smoke. He introduced me to artists like Circa Survive, Mars Argo, and Dance Gavin Dance. He was the first for sure autistic boy I ever dated, and, if I remember right, I was his first girlfriend. I loved his mom, but his younger sister absolutely hated my fucking guts - for literally - no reason. He was nice, until he wasn't. I gave him his first BJ, and he info dumped about communist stuff.

A few months in, this guy brought me to a venue that changed my life forever in Very Bad ways.

Eerily (or an omen), the first time I drove there, I was t-boned by a drunk driver, totaling my car.

That accident shook me like nothing really had before. I had a meltdown and begged my mom to let me drive her dark green Camaro to this new music venue that sounded really *really* cool, so I could hang out with people because I just really needed to let off the excess energy of the crash.

She, reluctantly, let me, and I arrived at a strip mall where a bunch of hipsters were smoking. It was called "the Modern Post". The Modern Post was also a hookah bar, and they hosted shows almost every night, or the same regulars would show up, and chain smoke cigarettes, get high, drink alcohol secretly in jumbo gas station cups, and a few folks hung out in the back all night.

I don't remember if someone there suggested it, or if I chose to on my own accord, but this was the first, and only time in my life, that I chain smoked cigarettes. Those shitty pink Camel #9s.

That very first night I was there, the most attractive punk guy I'd ever seen in my life, at the time, walked in, and I had one of those moments where it felt like time slowed down. He had a lip piecing and was generally just very nice to look at. (A few months later we made out at a party, but nothing more came from it because we just both decided we were better off as friends.)

A few days later, I came back with that same commie guy, and someone was having a birthday. (This was the first moment in my life I had met a vegan. I saw vegans as almost alien at the time. They had their falafel and looked so skinny, almost other-worldly. I couldn't understand them.)

Anyway, I don't remember why, but commie guy and I ended things. And I got a crush on a guy there (who, now, oddly enough, I found on TikTok about a year ago, and is popular on there for being a cute punk guy). Honestly, I never learned very much about the guy besides the fact he really liked Scott Pilgrim. But, one night, we were all in the back room of that venue and I was getting bored, so I wrote on my phone, "do you wanna go makeout in my car?" And he smirked at me all cute, nodding his head, and then we both got a bit carried away, and we had sex there. It was very fast, and I didn't get off, as usual when it comes to having sex with cismen, most times.

As the small world of "The Region" would have it, Frankenstein ex's little sister was also there. We were all a few years older, and we actually ended up becoming okay friends for a bit there. A few of us would go out and drink far too much. Once, as a guy drove, I puked out his truck window. Despite the joke stoner friend made, I had in fact began to develop bad drinking habits. (However, at the time, I certainly did not know *why* I only ever drank around others in public.)

One lucky day, around this age, I arrived at my campus during a tabling event for some student organizations. As I walked near one of the tables, someone there chatting caught my eye. He was talking to a coworker, behind the university newspaper table. I notice he was a little awkward (but, in a charming way) with anime hair. I was immediately attracted to this guy and decided to approach them to "talk about the newspaper", when, really, I just wanted to ++++ him. We had immediate chemistry, and he asked me if I had any writing experience. I replied, "I did", and he asked me if I wanted to work for them. That tabling event for PUC student organizations was nearly over, so he invited me to the newspaper office to talk with me more about "the position".

By the time we got up to the university newspaper office, I was completely convinced that he was actually just hiring me into my first journalist position. And I did write, so I was like, why not? Meaning, because of social standards of job decorum, despite my attraction to him, I'd lost the plot. Which is why, by the time it was just him and I, alone in the office, when he asked me "Are you sure you came up to me to ask about a job?" I said "Yes, I'm sure," and I took the job. (And, also why, it wasn't until 7 or 8 years later that he disclosed to me, his side of things. I was absolutely oblivious to the fact that when he asked me that, he was subtly checking in with me, implying that he knew that I only came up to the table because I was interested in him, not a job.)

Anyway, the university newspaper gave new writers a short trial period. So, I did write a couple pieces for them, and then I didn't anymore. And, honestly, I don't remember how it went down.

But newspaper friend and I stayed in contact, and our dynamic remained sexually tense for years. Yet, nothing physical ever happened between us. Mostly because that was around the time I was already within the most traumatizing, and stereotypically undiagnosed autist, arch of my life: the manic pixie dream girl era. No identity, only vibes, alcohol, and what cismen projected onto me.

And by sexual tension, I mean, I made prolonged eye contact with him and laughed, except, also, a large part of my being *the bad guy* in this era, instead of having sex, was me thinking that I was flirting with them by saying something funny, when, turns out, I was saying something insulting. (Sexual tension newspaper friend and I still stay in contact, even though over the years we had many a falling out [mostly because he knows me better than anyone, even though I masked who I am as *the bad guy* for -- quite literally – the first decade of us getting to know each other...And, yes, I explained everything and big apologized to him after I realized I've always been autistic]).

Because, unfortunately, after my lifetime of observations, much of what cismen call "flirting" is mean. So, truth be told, I have a hella bad gauge of where flirting stops and bullying even begins.

I never understood how anyone else ever knew the rules of flirting ever since I was a teen. I have distinct memories of some pool parties where I'd be there, self-conscious, seeing people playing horse, or splashing each other with the right amount of water, and just not being able to compute.

(How's an autist supposed to learn to flirt inside cultures that romanticize and sexualize abuse?!)

A few weeks later, Scott Pilgrim guy started dating another girl, and I called it a lost cause. He was honestly a superficial jerk, anyway. And like birds of a feather, he had friends that were too. There was a real small group of guys who he hung out with there. They were the kind of guys I learned (that apparently exist?) who like to take a bunch of Vyvanse and write business plans. They all attended a high school about four times the size of mine, a few towns South of Munster.

One of his friends was kind of funny, but not my type. He liked ska **wayyy** too much. I only saw him as a "friend", but this guy had other plans. One night he and two of his guy friends, that I barely knew, come over to my apartment on a day I hadn't eaten. I was uncomfortable having all three of them over at the apartment that my parents paid for, but I tried to pretend like I wasn't.

That night, I drank two bottles of wine, black outed, and he raped me while his friends were right in my living room. It was only a one-bedroom apartment. His friends were bold enough to make mac n cheese from my pantry, leave pots and pans dirty in my sink, and then (those fuckers) stole my Modern Warfare II. Again, all I have from being raped are a few polaroid-ish clipped memories of being in my own shower with him. Another with him on top of my mattress on the floor. I woke up next to him wearing his sweater. As soon as I woke up, I tore it off, and kicked him out into my living room, disgusted. I didn't know what to do or say about it. All I had at the time was some of that shitty inflatable furniture. A chair, a couch, both deflating. So, I forgot. At the time, I didn't know that you can't consent to sex when blackout. I blamed myself and forgot. (There was a 'friend" I had in my early twenties when I was working at Spencer's who used to cut and dye my hair. I refuse to mention more because she dated him even though he raped me.)

For some reason what stuck with me the most from that sexual violence, other than the fact he and his friends tried to claim that "I wanted it" (which is definitively and legally an impossibility because, again -- I was black out drunk -- I cannot consent to sex when I am blackout drunk), is the look of those used mac n cheese pans in my sink. I was completely and totally nauseated by them. I think it was just the complete and utter lack of consideration for my life, paired with the fact I'd already been vegetarian that one year at Ball State, and became lactose intolerant from it. But I stopped being vegetarian, and over the years was already becoming increasingly disgusted by the worsening quality of meat. The consistency of meat always mattered to me a lot. Just like when I was a child, I basically only ate meat if I was able to forget it was ever an animal. If I got a reminder that it ever was (cartilage, too much fat, bones, or veins) I always lost my appetite. It was the process of making it into a non-animal product that made me forget and it edible to me. I knew I needed to undergo a different process too, in order to forget this guy "friend" r***d me.

And you know what I did to forget? The next night, I went out. I thought I could drink away the fact I got r***d without anything bad happening. I don't remember what I did that night, but unfortunately, by the end of the night another friend of Scott Pilgrim guy came home with me.

!!! The following passage contains content about sexual violence !!!

This guy was very conventionally attractive. Very sharp jaw. He easily did the most stimulants of them all. He almost always wore clothes of this one skate brand. The last thing I remember is on the way back, he insisted on buying a handle of Martini & Rossi wine at Walmart. After we drank, I blacked out, and he raped me just like his friend. I have one memory of us on my carpet.

A Decade to Clean

December 2011:

How
Does
one

Clean
A body

Defiled

Within
it's Own
Shower?

--

Where
Then
Is
Safe
To clean
Him
Off/ut
Of
You?

—-

December 2021:

Last night
I somatic
Danced,
Sobbed,
Flailed,
Rocked,
And shook
Free of the
Night he
Came over.

—-

One of my
rapists fell
skydiving,

broke every
bone in his
body & had
to relearn
how to walk.

—-

The U.S.
Legal
System
Could
Never
Be

So
Just.

I remember being afraid that I caught an STI, or worse, became pregnant. But all I could do was get tested, and then wait. (Because what was I supposed to do? The U.S. doesn't criminalize the vast majority of sexual violences. And that's not all, there are also lawyers dedicated to dragging sexual violence survivors through shit, specifically, to ensure rapists win lawsuits. It would've both been a waste of my time to come forward and hella retraumatizing to pursue -- for nothing.)

The legal system in the U.S. does not criminalize the vast majority of sexual assaults because, as I discuss in "Requirement Politics" the system was designed by and to benefit the same group that to this day commits the most sexual assaults. To see the extensive statistics about all of that, again, see that companion piece. Shortly after this creature feature double feature in my early-2011 self, I moved my mattress from the bedroom into my living room and built a whimsical fortress that stayed up there for quite a long time. The thing that people never tell you after you get r***d twice one night after another is that you have to keep living your life. It's like cancer in that way. I binge watched shows, movies, and played video games, since my TV was right there next to my mattress on the floor. I did the best that I could with what I had, inside a blanket fort.

I have fond memories from then, getting home drunk, and binging many Steak n Shake fries.

Not too long after this, I was still going to that venue because what else was I supposed to do? This was everyone I knew at the time, and I love going to shows with every fiber of my being. I had met many seemingly really cool people there, and I wanted to hang out with them, despite the two incidents of black out violence the men at this fucking place had already inflicted on me.

The only other guy I hung out with invited me and another friend over to his house to hangout once. I thought to myself, this couldn't possibly go wrong. There is a girl here with us, I am in the clear. That day they introduced me to the show Weeds, and we marathoned it and hung out.

!!! The following passage contains content about sexual violence !!!

I decided to sleep over there because I wasn't alone with this guy, and I was sure nothing bad was going to happen. I mean what could he do? This other AFAB person and I had safety in numbers (I thought). No, the next morning I was woken up to his hand between my legs. I had no way of knowing how long this had been happening because I had been fucking asleep. I was so completely and uttered frozen by it. That was the first time a violation like that happened to me.

I trusted this guy as if I would be safe with another AFAB person right there next to me, but no. I woke up to him touching me in my sleep. Ever since, when I can, I sleep with a pillow between my legs. That's how much that particular event fucked with my psyche, even over a decade later. If it hasn't already been made clear, most every time I spent going to the Modern Post, or hanging around people who went there, it somehow became another absolute fucking nightmare.

!!! The following passage contains content about a sexually violent serial killer !!!

Shortly after that, I reconnected with a friend from high school, and we would go to this diner in the area that was open 24/7. We'd hang there and drink the absolute worst quality diner coffee.

One night, we went to her parent's house (for the first / last time) and for some reason we settled on watching this one horrific documentary about that BTK serial killer. For anyone that doesn't know, that was a serial killer who would break into AFAB folk's homes Bound, Torture, and Kill them. But while he did that, he would also feed them live animals and sexually assault them.

As you can imagine, after those four described acts of violence I had lived through at the hands of men in my life who claimed to either "love me" or at least be a "friend" of mine, I wanted to do whatever I could to not contribute to additional needless acts of cruelty, that make any being feel like I have been made to feel. After finishing the BTK documentary, the friend of mine and I made a pact to go vegan because it was so fucked up. I was working Christmas shift at Spencer's Gifts at the time. So, I figured if I could withstand eating vegan while attempting to work a holiday shift at the mall -- I could be vegan -- *anywhere*. And now, it's fourteen years later, and I still am because the more that I learned about industrial animal agriculture and the health benefits of veganism, the more it just felt right to me. This was also what started me on my path to feminism, reading books by Carol J Adams: Animals & Women; The Sexual Politics of Meat.

Eventually, I met another guy from the town directly east of my hometown. He was cute, a little awkward, and funny sometimes, but also kind of a chauvinist. One day he bought me a rose that I put on my blanket fort. We had a fling, but he was looking for someone to get married to, and I never want to get married. I knew his friend group already because I'd hung out with them when I was younger, and almost dated another one of them when we first met (because this friend group is -- hands down -- some of the funniest people I've ever met in my whole fucking life, and it's undeniably attractive.)

Anyway, we all went camping once in fling guy's family camper. We had sex all over that thing. Later that night we had sex in the campground bathroom. It ruled. Again, this guy never got me off. Having sex with cismen is like baseball: never worth the hype.

After a while, I finally got sick of working at Spencer's, since the pay wasn't worth it, and I quit. Really, my last straw was they added a looped dub step playlist that seemed to last -- FoReVeR.

November 11, 2011 (11.11.11) was the long-awaited pre-release of Elder Scrolls: Skyrim. I have been playing Elder Scrolls games since Morrowind. And Oblivion: Shivering Isles is my all-time favorite game, so this was a really big deal for 21-year-old me. I arrived after one of my final Spencer's shifts to find the line already quite long. I readied myself to wait quite a while, when I noticed some weirdo eating a rotisserie chicken on the sidewalk. He had a group of friends with him, and I don't remember how we got to talking, but we did. One of them was very tall and he looked familiar in a way I couldn't quite describe. He had a very goofy personality, that he would use against you to make himself feel better. While he spoke, he made very exaggerated motions with his long arms, and had facial expressions to match. Eventually, we all got our video games, and I don't remember how, but, eventually, I was inside goofy guy's messy room, looking for clues to who he was, what he liked, and we looked through his Spotify on his laptop.

It was getting late, so I decided to go home, and as I reached for the handle of his front door, in the meekest voice, he asked, "will I ever see you again?" I looked back, sort of confused by his directness, and I don't remember what I said. For some years after, I wondered how the next few years would've been if he didn't ask, and I just left, and never came back to his parent's house.

You know that flying saucer ride at circuses where you go inside and it starts spinning, and your entire body gets stuck to the inside of its walls? That's exactly like what my next three years became, spending nearly every day and night at his parent's house. I sometimes wonder what I would have spent that time doing if I hadn't been such a parented orphan. As I disclosed in these first two chapters, hopping from friend's house to friend's house was truly just subconsciously second nature to me by the time that I'd reached his parent's door. He started out so sweet to me.

And so, I became curious to find out who he might be, because he seemed unusually familiar in a way I couldn't describe. Empty, always trying to fill the air with something to distract from that.

He kept a lot of stuff around him, and I learned later, almost always another person. He too was a huge horror movie fan. But he took it much farther than I ever did. He liked the really extra sick shit. Bookshelves lined with serial killer picture books. Like, he really invested in the gruesome.

Most of the time, beside his mattress on the floor, his room looked like a tornado ran through it. And in many ways, it did. He decorated his bedroom with nick-nacks, album, and movie posters.

Regrettably, he knew how to hook into me. From that question at his door, like spores, he grew inside. Meanwhile, I learned all his mannerisms. We shared a tone of voice, smirk, and his bed like a mirror. We were opposite dimensions, who could never mentally meet through thick glass.

We had an undeniable chemistry that didn't need to be vocalized because it sat between us daily.

I forget when I started sleeping over at his house, but it was like we were a couple of animals. I think that if we were born into a lifetime before language, we probably would've faired just fine.

Sooner or later, he learned of my drinking and incentivized me to get sober, unlike anyone else

I'd been around up until that point. In a sense, I have him to thank for that because he did incline me to exist for a year with no booze. But, for years, whenever I was at his house, I lived off of mostly spare pretzels in his parent's pantry. Sometimes I would stow away mandarins from my parents' or grab Chinese food. (This continued my lifelong complicated relationship with food.)

He didn't take care of himself well, and neither did I. I felt his emptiness and I laid with him in it. His mom did his laundry. Some days I cleaned his room. Other days, maybe his mom did. He played video games that he'd buy on her credit card, and I would watch him play them. One day he dropped his iPhone and the screen cracked, so he destroyed it, and she bought him a new one.

After that day, it was like a switch flipped in him, and he realized I would watch him do bad things and not say anything to him. As I had with many past people, I enabled his behavior. He seemed to want to test the ground of how far our chemistry and my bad boundaries would go...

One 4th of July night, he contacted me, asking me to pick him up from his family's holiday party. I did because, obviously, I wanted to go lay around his house with him and do nothing. I don't remember how it happened, but once I pulled up to his parent's house, we had our first kiss. He said something to the effect of, he just, "had to know what it was like," because the chemistry.

Once we got settled in, we were figuring out what to watch, as usual, and he said he had a horror movie he wanted to show me called August Underground. He said it was a fake snuff film, and the creators were prosecuted because they were accused of actually murdering the people acting in the film because it looked so life-like. I'd seen my fair share of fucked up shit in my day, so I thought to myself, alright, that's fine, this is just some gimmick, like how bad could it really be?

!!! The following passage contains content about sexual violence !!!

We had laid on one of his couches to watch a movie together before, but the energy was different since the kiss we had in the car. I got a little wine in me as well, and we started watching this movie. He asked me if he could give me a massage, and I was like, yeah, absolutely. I often gave him back massages, and he sometimes gave them back to me, always for a shorter period of time.

It didn't take long for the film to live up to its namesake, but I started to notice he enjoyed it way too much. Like, this wasn't the first time that I'd watched a horror movie with a guy before and he tried to put the moves on me. But this was distinctly different. The more snuff-film like this movie got, the more turned on he got. I'll never forget that at one point he literally said, "if they fuck that stab hole, I'm going to lose it." This guy put me into an impossible position mentally, and he knew what he was doing, in doing exactly what he did. He'd seen these movies before.

Remember, this was pre-Me Too era. And this was someone I grew to trust, who proceeded to show me a film that was as close to a real snuff film as possible, sexualizing it and touching me. I had absolutely no idea what to do or how to feel about it. So, I just didn't. In hindsight, it was a kind of sexual violation I have never seen described before. I guess he got what he wanted, he trauma-bonded me to him for years. It was the most confusing dynamic of my entire life thus far. On one hand, I had intense chemistry with him. But, on the other, I sure as fuck did not sign up for something like that. Thankfully, nothing like that ever happened again, but it hung over me.

Not to long after that, we did finally have sex. The first time we did it was really intense, almost primal. I helped him explore his fetishes and related aspects of his sexuality he was curious about. At the time, he identified as a man, and I'm not sure if he still does, but, if I'm honest, our sex was always gay. He may not see it that way, and it reinforced the cisheteronormative orgasm gap because I didn't ever get off (since, obviously, my needs were not a priority for him, like most every cisman I'd ever been with in my life then), but in other ways, it was queer as fuck.

!!! The following passage contains content about sexual violence !!!

Other times, he was very coercive. And those times were by definition, rapes. Any "sex" I had to be "talked into' was a rape. (Again, I experienced many sexual violences at this point, so I just froze. Meaning, he's responsible for times he coerced me into anything sexual, but I believe that in sexually violent landscapes, without comprehensive sex education, this violence is "normal".)

As time went on, empty guy interwove our new trauma-bonded intimacy with a potent strain of cruelties, that he seemed intoxicated by, and thus, compelled to do. At strange times, he would use little things he learned about me, like knives. It was like he had fun by hurting me. As if, he needed to take me down a peg because tearing me down made him forget his emptiness inside.

On an increasingly regular occasion, he argued in circles, until I cried, and then he'd gaslight me.

He appeared to take joy in asking me a question, and then laughing at me, as if he wanted me to think that nothing I had to say had historical validity or basis behind it. His bites were venomous.

But I was immune to his poison. I was like his snake handler, with antidote running in my veins.

Around this time, I went out for a drink to catch up with debt friend for the first time in years, and she told me about this thing called "financial domination" where all you have to do is talk shit to men who ask for it, and then they pay you. She said, "I think you'll be really good at it". I said, something like "bet" and I signed up for the site she told me about, and I *was* good at it. It was around 2012, so most people did not know this existed yet, and the market was not yet oversaturated. That summer, I made a couple thousand dollars between gift cards and donations without ever doing anything besides mostly just talking to older men and them wanting to spoil me for doing so. This experience truly showed me how frivolous the global economy is, and that economic disparity, in a world where men are willing to fork over thousands this way, is bullshit.

Empty guy knew that I did this and was mostly like "get your bag" but also acted kind of strange about it. I did research about what felt like new entire universes of fetish and kink communities. I met so many really badass people who were embracing their sexualities after lifetimes of shame. It was truly one of the most eye-opening and empowering experiences I could've ever imagined. This was when I learned about men wasting femme domme's time and my hard no on race play.

One day, empty guy took me to a popular comic/game shop in the area, and we chatted with the owner. The owner was the one who first suggested I dress like Ramona Flowers for

Halloween (which I did for like six years in a row). Anyway, a few months later, I ended up working there. I went to empty guy's parent's house to share it with him because I thought he'd be happy for me.

Instead, he told me that I didn't get the job because of my qualification, but because I had boobs. He had the nerve to say I took the job from him because "he'd wanted to work there for years".

By the time I was hired there, we were regulars playing casual MTG, buying comics, etc., yet his alleged desire to work there *somehow never came up to me* until it was a knife, used to stab me.

I would feel him slice, and then I'd lay with him because I'd already felt nothing for years. At least with him I felt something. I was sober, and I felt something. He was painful, and I felt him. (As someone with alexithymia [difficulty recognizing and expressing my own emotions], hyper-empathy, and interoception [hunger, temperature, etc.] issues, I often don't know how to identify what sensation happens in my body until it has become so intense, I can no longer ignore it.)

I also didn't stop to question why someone, who acted so sweet, and I had spent so much time with, could treat me like this because I was long accustomed to my "loved ones" mistreating me. Besides, I was mirroring him as much as he was doing this to me. So, it's more complicated, too.

This leads me to the most challenging realization of my having spent so much of my life living as *the bad guy*. First is, due to my life of masked autism and trauma, I enabled his bad behaviors (like I had others way before him) and no boundaries to protect me. Second is that me being *the bad guy* didn't qualify as my "own" identity, as much as it was mirroring his outward behavior.

There are people who hate seeing and talking with a mirrored version of themselves. That means, there is a significant chance that I made him feel the way he made me feel, as well. Yet, that is what many autists do to survive. No wonder studies show non-autistics discriminate against us. This society defaults every discrimination as features. Autists are ostracized, formally Dx or not.

Empty guy's heartless commentary aside, that game shop job did turn out to be a total nightmare.

I mainly worked at the shop a few non-negotiable days: one weekday, Fridays, and Saturdays. On that weekday I would mainly help the owner put away comics for subscribers and restock. Fridays

I would help run the Magic the Gathering tournaments and learned the micro-economy. Then, Saturday nights I would most often work entirely alone, organize and watch TV shows.

The longer I worked, the more I realized the vast majority of customers had already made up their opinion of who I must be by the time they walked up to the counter. I was constantly talked down to as if I couldn't possibly know anything about my literal job: Magic the Gathering cards, miniatures, or really *anything*, simply because I was a femme presenting person with blue hair.

The longer I worked there, the more of a verbally abusive asshole the owner also became to me. He had a kid who was autistic, who he was absolutely terrible to, and he was projecting a lot of textbook internalized ableisms at me. He expected perfection, the first time, and made it clear.

One day a customer had a seizure and I had to call 911 and I stroked his hair until they arrived. Another, I spent a few days color coordinating, thousands upon thousands of, magic cards. My main coworker was a friend of his who was the official judge of our Magic tournaments, and the owner didn't treat him right. I felt bad for him. We all deserved better than how the owner acted.

Beware Wolf

One Friday night, I was running the tournaments
as usual, and all the regulars were there, but
someone new, that kind of stuck out like a sore
thumb, also showed up. He had a long beard,
looked like he was probably in his thirties, and
showed up to play draft. For anyone that isn't
familiar with MTG, those are games where
people are handed packs of Magic cards and then
open them one at a time, pass around and pick
cards to build a deck, and battle for cash prizes.
Anyway, this guy kept looking at me, and was
obviously kind of shy, so I tried to make him feel
welcome in the shop, as much as I would anyone
else new, who I could tell didn't know anyone.
He ended up coming back the next day when I
was working alone at the shop, and he stayed
talking to me nearly the entire night. That was
when I learned he was from Philadelphia and was
currently traveling around the country to paint
people's portraits, entirely funded on Kickstarter.

He was a bisexual, poly, crust punk who
allegedly co-owned a game shop himself back
home. I had never met anyone like him before.
As he traveled he ran a blog, and also recorded
his travels within a Tumbler, that always included
photographs he took of local hiking trails along
the way. I hadn't been hiking for a quite while at

the Indiana Dunes, and so he invited me to go with him.

I need to make one thing clear, before I proceed. Beyond my stereotypically autistic naivety, during this point in my life, I had already lived through an incredible amount of trauma, and, mostly, at the time did not have a home or anything worth living for. In short, I did not care if I lived or died. So, all of this considered, I agreed to go with this strange crust punk to the dunes the following day. He picked me up from my parent's house in the station wagon he traveled in.

He acted like he respected the fact that I was vegan, and he loved to talk a lot. In fact, he did most of the talking from the point he picked me up from my parent's house, and I just listened.

At this point in my life, I was so very accustomed to men who talked and did not let me get a word in edgewise. He had a kind of nerdy older charm to him, that was relatively attractive in a way that was new to me. I was interested to learn about his life, and all the alternative ways he lived. I'd never met anyone who lived these ways. We arrived at the dunes and began the hike.

His first major red flag, besides never letting me get a word in edgewise, occurred shortly after we walked on this first trail. Maybe a minute in, there were a couple of older ladies who were approaching us, walking in the opposite direction. And, after moving out of the way to let them walk by the trail, he grabbed me, suddenly, pulling me into him and kissing me, grabbing my ass. I later realized, it was like he really wanted these two older ladies to see him treat me this way. I was so taken aback by his abruptness, that it hadn't registered to me, that I might be in danger.

We saw a little enclave off to the side, just a bit forward, with flowers and some butterflies. He took some pictures of them for his blog. I didn't think anything of it all. It was around 11 am when we arrived, so the day was young, and I thought to myself as he kept talking and we kept walking, "okay, bird, worse comes to worse, this was a weird encounter, and we'll go home." Except, we just kept walking, and he just kept talking. He would keep telling me about his DnD campaigns, and games that he played from his own game shop. I asked him questions about his life, and he answered them in increasingly long monologues, as if this entire trip was about him.

Eventually, we stopped to eat lunch in a little tree surrounded area with a picnic bench. He kept talking, and talking, and talking, and talking. I ate some random fruits, seeds, and fig nutans. The long minutes, turned to long hours, and there we were, still walking on these trails. It wasn't until it started getting dark that I started to see this man differently. There was one particular long trail back to where his station wagon was, that it occurred to me: This is a strange man. I very well might be in grave danger. I had been looking at his face, nearly all day, but now, when I saw his face, all I could see was a werewolf. For at least another fifteen minutes I walked alongside this strange man, who I could not stop seeing as a werewolf. Finally, we got to his car. I felt a moment of relief, thinking I was about to go home, and this could all be simply a memory.

But, as soon as we arrived at his car he said that he had trouble driving at night, and that we'd have to sleep nearby instead. My mind panicked and stomach dropped into an abyss. I was at the Indiana Dunes, the one place in the entire Region where I had no phone signal -- whatsoever. And I was with an actual real-life werewolf who claims he cannot drive at night and is holding me captive against my will. Every cell in my body knew I was now in danger, and I needed to do whatever I needed to do to just stay alive. I needed to appease this werewolf if I wanted to live.

So, that's what I did. He drove us to a parking lot by the lake. I realized I was near the end of my period, and I had exactly one tampon with me. He suggested we go swimming before sleeping in the back of his station wagon. I said I didn't have a bathing suit, so he let me borrow a pair of his shorts. As I changed, he tried to peek at me, and I ran away. He acted like invading my privacy was a funny little game, but I was already so very uncomfortable with being made to sleep with him in his station wagon, that it just made me physically sick to see him at all. I couldn't let him know that, though. The entire time with him was a game of not letting him know real thoughts.

Lucky for me, I had already mastered never allowing, especially men, to know who I was, or my thoughts. This wasn't the first cisman I had to listen to talk, and fawn like I cared what he said. I was an old pro at doing exactly that. If I needed to do it for an undisclosed period of time, I could do that no problem. So, after I'd changed, I walked over to the sand. Next thing I knew he picked me up, hoisted me over his shoulders, like a was a rag doll, and ran us into the lake. It was at this moment that I knew I did not stand a chance against this adult man, if I needed to put up a fight. He demonstrated to me that he could lift and run with me as if I was made of fucking Styrofoam.

I had been in Lake Michigan many times. Sometimes middle school friends and I would go to the beach at night at the Whiting beach, smoke, drink, and skinny dip, in this exact lake shore. When I was a kid, I took field trips there, learned then that if I wasn't careful while wave jump riding, the tide could easily take hold of me and slam my tiny, body face first into the seafloor.

I knew what weightless danger felt like, and that night a large part of me wished the lake would instead take ahold of me and mercy kill me, before whatever this crusty old cisman had planned. We got out of the water, and he bragged significantly more about his Kickstarter campaign. For at least another hour before we walked back to the wagon, I told him whatever he wanted to hear.

Once we got back to the station wagon, we got inside, and crawled into the back area where it was clear that this strange man lived nearly his entire life for months and months and months. At night, he had covers for the windows made of various tattered sheets, for privacy and sun. I don't remember what he talked about as I drifted off to sleep, but he successfully tired me out that day.

!!! The following passage contains content about sexual violence and false imprisonment !!!

I don't remember what woke me up in the middle of the night. It might have been, that I heard a rhythmic beating sound. It might have been him touching me. But I rolled over to find him, pants down, and jerking off, wildly right next to me. In my half-asleep state, I'll never forget that I said to him, "this is your house, I'm just sleeping in it" and I rolled back over to go to sleep. It was at that moment that I knew I was in absolute undeniable danger, and I realized I might lose my life.

It wasn't my first night being woken up to a form of sexual trauma at the hands of a cisman. As I laid there, before I fell back asleep, I came to terms with the fact this werewolf could murder me. I'd seen enough horror to know people cooler than me had been left as mere bodies in the woods. So, I made a pact to myself right then, I would outsmart this fucking werewolf, and get out alive.

The next day, I was alive, and it was rainy. He decided we should drive to a different area of the dunes and see a different segment of the beach. We played a Star Trek card game in the sand.

The entire day was a blur. He talked, I made it seem like I cared. I took in nothing of his words. Eventually, I disclosed I was on my period and that I needed to use the bathroom to pee and change my tampon. We got up, and walked back to the station wagon, and drove to the closest dunes bathroom. One of those outdoor bathrooms, with a surprising number of families nearby.

!!! The following passage contains content about sexual violence and false imprisonment !!!

I used the bathroom, and when I came back, he was in the back of the station wagon, horny. I knew I needed to do whatever he wanted me to, and acted as if I also wanted it so I might stay alive to see anyone I ever knew again, so, I went along with it. We made out, I was disgusted. He took his pants off, I was disgusted. He asked me to take my clothes off, and I was disgusted. He masturbated, I was disgusted. He told me he wanted to see me touch myself, and I was the most disgusted of all. I still had my tampon in, and I knew there were families with small children just outside the tattered cloth he called privacy screens in the parking lot of the dune's bathroom area. I was trapped in my own body, no phone signal or means of escape, at the whim of a sick fucker.

I'd experienced multiple sexual violations before, but never felt so fucking disgusting in my life. My mind couldn't quite compute an escape. Then it occurred to me, I had to make this guy think that I was interested in being with him. I was obviously what he wanted. Whoever he thought that I was, despite barely ever letting me get a word in between his fucking monologues. So, I needed to really play the part. I needed to figure out what this sick fucker was after, and fast. He finished, and we drove back to the parking spot that we'd slept in the night before. It was a rainy day, and he asked if I wanted to play some other game. I obliged because what option did I have?

!!! The following passage contains content about sexual violence and false imprisonment !!!

Next thing I knew, he wanted to go down on me. Again, I had a tampon in, but he said he really wanted to. I even tried to subtly talk him out of it, in a covert way that wasn't face threatening to his ego. I framed it as if he was so generous. I asked him, are you sure, because I'm leaving my tampon in. He replied he was sure because obviously my consent was his to decide at all times. It didn't matter what I thought about any of the assaults, I was basically just a live doll companion.

Once again, I found myself in a spot where the last barrier between me and some sick fuck was a tampon. Fortunately, this time the metaphorical cotton door was not bashed in when I was drunk. The door stayed closed. I told myself, as long as the door was closed, he hadn't gotten all of me.

I don't remember if he made me stay another night at the dunes with him or if we drove back to Munster. But either way, when we got back into town, I still was trapped in his van. There was a part of me that considered opening his station wagon, tucking, and rolling my way to freedom.

But this was no action movie, this was real life, and I didn't want road rash, on top of all else.

My mind was in a haze, and as far as I knew, I was convincingly playing the part of a person who not only wanted to be around this rapist, but also gladly did whatever he wanted me to do.

Ironically, he asked me what I wanted to do, and I told him, I wanted to change clothes, and grab some stuff from my house. He said he wanted to spend more time with me. I don't know if it was the ongoing intensive trauma of it all, or the fact that he already knew where I lived because he picked me up from my parent's house the first morning, but either way, I went in, changed my clothes, grabbed things, and went back out to him. I climbed back in his wagon, and he drove me to a Walmart parking lot nearby. Walmart let's people sleep there in RVs and shit. So, we went and restocked up on some food for the night. That night, he tried to convince me to move back to Philadelphia with him. To this day, I am convinced that if I had he would have sex trafficked me.

We stayed a night there in the Walmart parking lot, and then the next day, we said our goodbyes.

!!! The following passage contains content about sexual violence!!!

He planned to come back into the area. He would text me saying he "missed me", and I was so fucked up by it, that I continued to play the part. Eventually, he sent me a link to a cartoon series incestuous age gap erotica. He came back into the area once, and I told him "my feelings faded".

I didn't remotely know how to handle what he did to me. So, I just didn't handle it at all. I acted like it never happened for years. I told no one except a therapist eventually. She said, "Looks like you processed it well". (Against all odds, this year I tried to pursue a legal case against him, ten years later, but the lawyers didn't accept. I can barely afford to live anyway, so I can't afford to. I told a paralegal right before my office hours, between sobs, and then went in to be a professor.)

I continued to work at the game shop that I met this monster at, like nothing had ever happened.

I think the first thing I did was go back to empty guy's house and lie down on one of his couches.

At least when I laid there with him, I didn't have to think. At all the low, low price of being hurt.

"Lil' bird, Wake Up! Wake up, Lil' bird!"

I think maybe I woke up the time at work a real adult man asked me a question, only to lure me into the game area, away from cameras, and proceed to ask me a lot of questions about my feet.

Or maybe it was the time I went to the gas station, and an elderly man pulled into the parking lot, drove his truck up near my car, and started to watch me pump gas while he masturbated, and I tried to yell at him to go away. Maybe, *that* was *my final straw* with cisheterosexism...............? Maybe it was the therapist I went to and told about werewolf guy and him false imprisoning me. Maybe I was just getting a little too tired of not having anything worth living for after 24 years?

Either way, in my coursework, I started to learn significantly more about societal problems and critical theory. So, after years of lying around with empty, I decided to start pushing back at his mirror. I decided to have my own fun. I became a fun house mirror -- if you will. He hated that.

No matter what the catalyst, I was already a few years into my bachelors in sociology. Whereas empty guy was pursuing his in psychology, at a different university nearby. If we did talk those days, which we rarely did, our disagreements went far beyond the usual disagreements between psychology and sociology. He argued in circles, made ahistorical and racist comments, as if they were fact, and never listened to what I said with any respect. In fact, if I pointed out something I know to this day is true (as a specialist now in this material), he would insult me for it. I became exhausted by him. This was around the time other people started to talk to me about his behavior.

I was always around other regulars from the shop, being that I worked during every major night. And I really started enjoying their company, even though a lot of the patrons needed deodorant. One guy, in particular, I became rather close with, and he started telling me I deserved better. He saw how empty guy treated me, and he wanted me to know that I shouldn't have to deal with it. Healthy treatment and respect were novel ideas for 24 y.o. me at the time, but I thought, why the hell not? Lemme try that for a change! Either way, one thing, for sure: I was Bern'd the fuck out.

Part Two.
Bern'd Out

Chapter Three. You Mean…I Can't Work/Drink This All Away?

Often times I've thought about how much easier my life might have been if I wasn't ever able to pass my struggles off and hide them. But then I remember how fucking ableist this world is, and realize that that's a lie that I've told myself to feel better. Lies, often times, feel so Very Good.

Other times they feel **Very** Bad. Like, for most of my life, I've been made to feel absolutely indescribably terrible about myself. No matter how hard I tried, or whatever I tried, it was never enough. It was much easier not to think about most of my early life. It was like my brain blocked it out until I knew I was autistic. Until learning that, I have lived so deeply miserably in ways I couldn't begin to understand. I never want anyone to feel the ways that I've been made to feel.

And to be honest, the few times I went to therapy barely ever helped that misery fade. Whenever I've gone to a therapist, this is how it's went:

More often than not, I go to one appointment, I unload all the things that I needed to get off my chest. I therapeutically sob. They ask me what my goals are, I have no idea. I just really needed someone to hear all this shit. Many times, a therapist would say, "it sounds like you have a lot on your plate." Like, no kidding. When I got older, a few told me "You know, you don't need to talk to your parents anymore, if you don't want to". And "that was abusive behavior that you didn't deserve". And I am forever grateful to them for that. But to be honest, what was most useful to me was that the handful of therapists I went to before my PhD, would validate things that I already knew. After learning *what* and *how* abuse and trauma were, I knew I had experienced a great deal of both. I learned that I am very good at balancing a lot on my plate and making it look like my plate is empty at the same time.

I guess I have my stereotypically autistic alexithymia, interoception issues, and the occasionally lesser emotive disposition to thank for that, in certain ways. In other ways, I was often told that I am intimidating and cold. Many times, in my life, later on, people would disclose to me that, without knowing me, they'd look at me and think that I was a bitch. I had absolutely no idea why anyone was intimidated by me. But apparently the way that I understood myself, in early life, was dramatically different than the disposition that I was presenting to the world.

Surely, I will never understand the full complexities of the way that that worked. And honestly that's probably for the best. In many ways, people not wanting to be around me in my early life also probably protected me from even more bullshit. In other ways, my demeanor hadn't protected me from experiencing non-statistically autistic amounts of discriminations, abuse, and sexual violences.

From what I hear, this is a common thing for autists. In hindsight, I now realize that in my 20s, I would teeter at random points between masking my autism and not masking my autism. My mask would fall off, and I would pick it back up, and try to put it back on like nothing happened. I would try to glue it on to last for the day, like my dad and dentures (he got from lack of care).

Relatedly, plenty of folks at different points in my life have asked me: So, how did you get into graduate school, bird? Whenever they do, my script that I say goes a little something like this...

That One Time I Thought I Could Work/Drink This All Away

One day during my junior year of college, I arrived to campus to find a tabling event. There was a woman behind the table who I was immediately attracted to. Her smile was unbelievable. I was absolutely pulled to her (a pattern, I guess). I went to talk to her, and it turned she was behind the environmental club table. I learned she was from Columbia, and here pursuing a degree in (I think) environmental science. We hit it off. She invited me to not only join the environmental club, but to also attend a Greenpeace leadership summit in Virginia. She was chosen to be a leader at the summit, and she thought I would really enjoy it. I would've followed her anywhere.

Doing something like this was completely outside of my character, but I agreed to do it. And little did I know at the time, this queer crush would go on to change the entire course of my life. But before I actually went, and all days leading up, almost every part of me wanted to bail. I was absolutely terrified to go. (My ability to live day to day is a constant struggle as a PDA profile autist. I was easily destabilized, and especially was then. I had absolutely no knowledge of the fullness of my own difficulties and/or any skills to regulate. I was running purely on this crush.

We hung out a number of times before we went to this leadership summit, and her smile stayed as beautiful as ever. She was absolutely brilliant, and there was no doubt in my mind she would go on to do incredible things. Her entire presence oozed that and was so incredibly inspiring to me. Then, I found out she was queer. I'd never been so happy. I thought "what are the odds...?" It felt like an actual Region miracle, after my lifetime of repressed comphet pairings I had lived.

We started seeing each other casually, and eventually we went to the Greenpeace leadership summit with another person from the club. Because she was a leader for the summit we arrived early, so she could get trained for it. And to do so, we went to Greenpeace's secret headquarters.

The only problem for my mind and I was, this route of travel was almost completely outside of my control, and I did not handle uncertainty and loss of control well then. There was one point at which we got lost and I felt like we weren't going to be found and (due to everything, I explained before), when I got scared or felt out of control at that age, I wasn't very enjoyable to be around.

After the main bus ride, we were on the side of a road in an area that I did not know, that didn't look safe, and we had all our belongings with us. In my mind, we were vulnerable sitting targets.

Luckily, she called one of her contacts from Greenpeace, and they came to pick us up in a very suspicious looking white van from the side of the road, and they drove us to their headquarters.

(I think they do this because they want secrecy about where the headquarters is located, but honestly, it was not accessible to someone who is autistic. It wasn't fair to me, and it wasn't fair to anyone around me that travel was handled this way, since accommodating people that are autistic is not the default setting. If disability accommodations were norm, I'd have been fine.)

Anyway, we eventually got to the headquarters, and there, I was finally able to shower and change clothes, after all the public transport. Despite my day-to-day struggles with general upkeep of my body, that process has always been like a mental reset for me. Afterward, it feels like my body is in cohesion and I am ready to exist in public. (This is a combination of my own sensory needs, and the gratification that I've learned I receive when I look most "presentable".)

One thing I forgot to mention about myself up until this point (somehow?) is that, besides reset showers, the way that I dressed my entire life had either been something I -- absolutely didn't care about -- or something that makes or breaks my ability to feel put together as a human being.

As anyone still here has read extensively, most of my life, I was not in my body, due to a deadly combo of repressed PDA autistic sensory/demand oversensitivity, as well as traumatizing sexual violence disassociation, AND alexithymia and

143

interoception issues. So, for the most part, when I started to care about how I dressed, I only cared about how it looked in the mirror. I've always understood the way I presented myself as a kind of geometry. It's like my own personal Euclid geometry. I know it when I see it, and it's a science. Meaning, I either have solved the problem, or it goes unsolved, and I feel terrible an entire day. (Now that, at 33, I have returned to my body full-time I am still dressing for my own personal style, and it first revolves around my comfort.)

Which is to say, I felt so much better after that fuckin shower. I still had no idea where I was going to sleep, but I felt like I could at least talk to the strangers. The strangers were very nice. We made a group meal. And I learned this was something that they just do, and it felt so right.

Like, they took turns with responsibilities and share them with the community, so no one takes on too much, and everyone gets a turn to care for one another. They made me feel so incredibly welcome. Most of their food was also vegan and they didn't treat it like it was a burden. That was just the default because they knew that it was better for the environment and because I was vegan, and they wanted to care for that. That was a rare time I never felt like a burden for my veganism by others. They accommodated this rather well the entire summit marking everything with little signs that said "vegan". (Even though, once, the signs for the quiche got accidentally mixed up and I ate an actual egg quiche for the first time in my life. But, as soon as they learned, they apologized, and told me, and I just got a bad headache. I had survived worse, so it was fine.)

The retreat was typical, and at the world's most beautiful place. It was my first time ever seeing a Virginia farm aesthetic morning. I had never seen grass, trees, and fog like this. It was like being inside a postcard of a peaceful countryside paradise. I immediately got the vibe that everyone else there was very successful. I felt completely out of place. As discussed earlier, I had put zero eggs into my K-12 education. These were college kids with helicopter parents from Washington, DC with resumes that go on to "be someone". Luckily, I didn't care about any of that. And I had spent my life around a variety of different social classes enough to blend in with them, despite our differences. I met so many really cool people. But as days went on, I noticed one quiet girl, who kept looking at me. She didn't talk very much, and I thought that maybe her first language wasn't English, or she was just very shy. I tried my best to be nice to her if it became relevant.

She was the kind of person that just kind of stuck out as not talking with anyone else, and so I was probably one of the few people who had even tried to say anything nice to her at all. But I spent time with everyone else. In fact, I made a small group of friends that were really incredible.

One of them was actually pursuing their media & communication bachelor's at Bowling Green.

At the time, I had never heard of it (like most universities in the entire world. And, mostly, that hasn't changed to this day). This person introduced me to the game banana grams, and after explaining to them that I have no idea what I was going to do with my bachelors in sociology, just from talking to me they recommended I pick up a minor in communication. Mind you, at the time, I was so terrified and uncomfortable with myself that I had put off taking a public speaking course. I didn't take public speaking until my junior year of college (the semester right before that one). I remember reading the textbook and thinking "this is what I want to be doing with my life". But I felt like I was too far along in my sociology bachelor's program to be able to just switch my entire degree. (By that time, I had already been accommodating myself to handle the workload of a typical bachelor's program and living off credit and the meager student loans each year, part time, about five years into a 6 1/2-year total, mostly self-scheduled, bachelor's degree.)

Because of this one serendipitous person's recommendation and explanation of communication to me, the entire course of my life changed. (I came back from that summit and spoke with my undergraduate advisor who was also the chair of the sociology department, who signed me up for a graduate level course in rhetoric. The professor was the dean of students, and she talked to me like I was someone who had things to contribute and should be listened to. More on this later.)

That *Other* Time I Almost Died

Anyway, every college kid attending this environmental leader summit, slept in an assigned cabin on the property. There were cots in them we got to choose, and most everyone slept in the same cot that they had the night before because that's where we each kept all of our belongings.

One day, my new group of friends and I went into the bathroom and found the quiet, shy girl writing poems with her own blood on the wall while muttering to herself. We responded to this event as anyone would, we went and told a leader of the summit, so they could do something.

We were freaked the absolute fuck out, for obvious reasons. As readers have seen in the first two chapters of this memoir, I had already seen shit before, and even as naive as I was, I knew this was *bad*. This woman caught wind of my having told on her, and from then on her vibe changed.

As I said before, sleeping arrangements of the summit were rather flexible, yet almost everyone remained in their same cot night-to-night to sleep. Well, after her "incident", I began to notice the very quiet blood poem girl who stared at me, was now also staring at me, with evil intent. It was like I could see her crafting a way to hurt me. And thanks to my pattern recognition, I also noticed she began moving one cot, closer, and closer to mine each night. With each day of this, I grew increasingly more uncomfortable. I began watching over my shoulder and making sure I wasn't alone. I made eye contact with her to let her know I was watching her. It was like staring at pure evil. The energy of her nefarious intent was so palpable to me, that I couldn't ignore it.

So, to do the cot math for y'all, from where she started sleeping, by day four of this retreat, she would've been sleeping directly next to me. And as soon as I saw that, I asked the same leader I told about the bloody poem wall situation if I could please move cabins. Luckily, they agreed.

It should be no surprise, because of the mental duress this person caused me each day since, an immediate sense of relief washed over me as soon as I wasn't sleeping in the same cabin as her.

And this was, despite the fact that, during the retreat, more likely than not because of my unrealized mini autistic meltdown on the way to the headquarters, combined with the fact, I started noticing my queer crushes chemistry with another one of the summit helpers, she had understandably closed the emotional door on me. (At the time then, it hurt me for reasons I had no way to fully unpack, realize, or articulate in any, way, shape, or form until realizing late-in-life, I'm autistic. I completely understand and respect her reaction to me, all things considered.)

Anyway, the next morning we were leaving the retreat. Everyone had their shit packed, and the way that it worked was, we were all going to go on some buses that took us to whatever other major forms of transportation we each needed to get back to our homes. All night I mentally prepared how I was going to ensure I kept at least one eye on this woman to make sure she didn't pull any *funny shit*. I deliberately got ready and arrived early to the bus. And made sure that as soon as we could board the buses, I put my suitcase in the bottom, and I got on the bus. Also to protect myself, I decided that I was going to sit in a window seat, and then put my feet up on the seat next to me, so I would only allow people I knew, thus, controlling who could sit next to me.

For a number of minutes, just like that, I kept an attentive eye on the entrance of the bus, seeing who was entering it, just waiting. The next thing that I knew, I saw bloody wall poem girl, who clearly looked for me, boarded, and stared piercingly at me, beginning to approach me. She then proceeded to use all her body weight to move my legs, forcing herself, to sit right next to me.

At this point, my blood ran cold. My adrenaline kicked in. As soon as she sat down, I saw her backpack was on her lap with a large Greenpeace pin on it (Many of which we were given at the retreat). Immediately after, she went for it, unpinned it, and pried the pin needle up. As soon as I saw that shit, I fought, and grabbed it from her hands so fast, saying "yeah, I'll be taking this!"

I have absolutely no doubt that if I had not won that struggle against her, she would have at least maimed me. I may not have both my eyes right now, she might've had plans to completely slit my throat, for all I know. All I know is, as soon as that happened, I said, "Absolutely Not, get the fuck up, sit somewhere else". And, defeated, she moved to sit somewhere else behind my seat.

As you can imagine, I was now absolutely buzzing with near death adrenaline, and no clue what to do. I had no idea how to tell anyone. So, I texted newspaper friend and told him exactly what just happened. Eventually, everyone else got on the bus, and it started moving. As I sat, texting, I remember watching the beautiful pasture disappear, and turn into Washington, DC cityscape.

Meanwhile, I physically shook for at least over an hour, sitting by myself, on high alert, looking back to where this evil woman was sitting, making sure they never got up to pull any more shit.

Eventually we all got off the bus, and unfortunately, this person was in the small group that was assigned to go to the same main lobby area where the bigger forms of travel to our homes were. Within this area, I made sure to get behind this woman, the entire time that she was still with us, so that I could watch her and know that she wasn't going to fucking attack me again. I was so distraught for my life, yet I told no one. And then she just left, and I never saw that fucker again.

So anyway, me and queer crush got on a greyhound, and we went back to the Region. On the way, I realized I didn't have anyone to pick me up. So, I called my mom to ask her to pick me up at the Gary greyhound station, over an hour before we arrived. By the time we did, she wasn't there. My mom forgot to pick me up. At this point, I was having a meltdown. No one around me knew what I had just lived through, and I looked like I was having a hissy fit, like a child whose parent forgot to pick them up at the age of 23. Thankfully, the woman picking up queer crush was willing to drive me and drop me off on campus where my car was, and I got home just fine.

That One Time I Was Reborn

As I said much earlier (before describing her attack), the next thing I remember is going to my advisor, who signed me up for that graduate course as a part of my new minor in communication.

Turns out, that Greenpeace leadership summit was mostly just a funnel for the organization to recruit and train their ongoing initiative the "Act for Arctic" campaign. So, I came back from it and started a chapter of the Act for Arctic campaign on campus through the environmental club.

I spent many days tabling for that, or the environmental club, on campus. And I met a lot of cool people that cared about the world during that whole experience. Thankfully, all my experience with retail gave me a practically iron will to table for a campaign that wasn't corporate bullshit.

That same semester I was in a social media campaign course, and it also somewhat helped me learn how to spread the word on social media sites for the campaign I was running. The course was kind of bullshit, if I'm totally honest. It was taught by someone who that same semester was in my graduate course. They weren't a very good instructor, but they did give me resources like Kahoot. They acted much more like an ad. consultant because, as I later learned, they also were.

About a month after I came back from the Greenpeace leadership summit I took another bus with the Sierra Club, Greenpeace, and a bunch of random cool hippies of all ages to the 2014 People's Climate March. There I learned, New York City wreaks like piss. Around this time, I had started to attend many various protests for different human rights violations and systemic oppressions.

So, anyway, around the age of 24, my parents and I moved into a condo for the first time since I was three, even though we had been "looking for a new house", practically, my whole f'ing life.

We moved in shortly before Thanksgiving. And I remember that, distinctly, only because my dad had a heart attack and died for a whole 15 minutes after eating a Thanksgiving meal at some of our extended family's house. His cardiologist was our old neighbor (the dad of the backyard boys). When my family was in the waiting room, I was texting empty guy and he was actually relatively supportive, if I remember right. I was absolutely distraught in a way that I only have been a few times in my life. The cardiologist was about to call him dead. Then, he came back to life -- completely unexplainably -- said this heart doctor. But he came back, and as far as we know, he didn't have any brain damage, despite the fact he was legally dead for 15 minutes and came back a nicer guy than he used to be, who could now eat significantly less salt on our watch!

So, anyway, when he was dead, me and my sister and my mom were in the hospital lobby in the middle of the night, and I was having an absolute fucking meltdown about the fact that my dad never took care of himself, despite knowing he already had medically high blood pressure for years, and that I couldn't believe he never listened. (Obviously, my autistic meltdown diatribe was not exactly what my mother or older sister wanted to hear when their husband and father were dying. But I'm an autist who intellectualizes things, and so that is what I fucking sobbed.)

Shortly after that, for the first real time, I told empty guy to fuck off and I quit the sexist game shop, both in the exact same day. The last day I worked, my first graduate course was that night. The sexist ass shop owner said something to me that was the final straw. So, after he finished yelling at me for fucking nothing, he went to the bathroom, and I walked out on his fuckin ass.

And so that's why I began working at the university newspaper again. But, this time, I went to the new editor-in-chief, and I pitched that the paper divide up what used to be the managing editor position (that as it was then, included three jobs worth of work), so I could be their new advertising manager. I had no experience in doing that. It worked purely because he either had pity for me or was persuaded by what I said. Either way, I did become their next advertising manager, and sold about $700 or $800 in advertising for a local bowling alley in our paper. That semester, I was enrolled in courses like "By and About Women" and "Women in America" by absolutely incredible professors who were supportive of me, stacking my personal and political know-how. I also continued to take graduate courses, as an undergraduate, and excelled in them.

My professors/mentors at that point in my life fully catalyzed me to build my self-esteem from nothingness into having an identity that I could -

for the first time in my life - be proud of. My first graduate level paper was about Emma Watson's, "He for She" campaign. I got a C on it, but I didn't let that grade deter me. I sat in that first graduate rhetoric class with actual grad. students and knew I had so much to learn from them and our professor because I did. And I did learn a lot from reading critical feminists and rhetoricians like Simone de Beauvoir, Kenneth Burke, and Mary Daly. I learned I had been thinking like a critical scholar and rhetorician, for a long time.

Yet I had been treated by people, studying psychology and sociology, as if my take on the world, built through language, was nonsense. Because of those professors, I learned that what I gained just from existing was insightful and valid. I learned that the field of communication was in its infancy, and that people who had thought like I had, have gotten paid for thinking and speaking like I did. From that moment on, I knew that I needed to do anything/everything I possibly could to put in work, so that I could do that too. No matter what it took, I needed to become who I was.

Semesters went by, where I still frequented going to empty guy's parent's house, sharing with him what I learned and then he would proceed to treat me like absolute fucking dog shit for it. But it was around then I stopped caring what he said. I learned that what he had to say had absolutely no historical validity to it. I learned that his lashing out at me was a "him" problem.

Lesson by lesson, critical reading upon critical reading, inside and outside of the classroom, I began to animorph from being his nearly full time live in fun house mirror, to "the bad guy".

That next interesting semester ended, and I enrolled in another grad. course in communication as an undergraduate student in sociology, after that. I researched and wrote about the exploitation of nail salon workers in different socioeconomic and racialized areas of the Midwest. I researched and wrote a personal narrative paper about my experience working at the sexiest ass game shop.

After being in a few classes that were all taught by that same professor who assigned me those reflection papers, they were supportive of me and helped expedite me into the communication M.A. program. I remember her asking me one day after our class, near the end of my bachelor's program, "Are you going to actually join our master's program?" and I asked back "I don't know, do you think I should?" And she replied, "What are you talking about?! Get in here!"

Another actual master's student at the time, who I had gotten to know from being in courses together, despite not being in the program yet, recommended I apply for the program's teaching assistantship to teach public speaking courses during the masters. That absolutely terrified me. But because of her encouraging me, I did. I remember going in for the interview for the position, physically shaking, and feeling my face and chest get so red I knew I had to have looked like a firetruck. I had zero teaching experience then, and I'd only just taken public speaking the year prior. I got a C. I remember telling her, "I think this would really help me. I think my anxiety might really help other students that have bad anxiety. And if I can do that, I want to help them."

The Bad Guy Strikes Back (It Me)

My identity began to actually form for the first time in my entire life. Shortly thereafter, I was asked to take part in a campus event called "That Takes Ovaries" where I read someone else's narrative of survival in front of an audience. That same semester, I wrote a paper about a new relationship that I started months earlier with someone who actually treated me with care for one of the first times in my life, around the end of my bachelors (he attended that "Ovaries" event and was hella supportive of me). To this day, he's one of the most incredible poets I've ever met.

After going to his house for the first time, I learned that he had an abusive upbringing. His dad would abuse his family if they didn't clean the house in the way that he demanded. So, his whole family hoarded. It was their way of empowering themselves to keep their home -- however they wanted. He was another regular from the game shop. He knew about empty guy because he was friends with him. He used to freeze and physically react uncomfortably from the sound of a fork scraping against a plate while we had meals. And it was something his family knew well about.

His entire family had textbook "neurodivergent" qualities. I loved them for that. At the time I didn't know they were "neurodivergent" qualities. They just reminded me of me and accepted me for who I was. Despite being more religious than me, they invited me to fellowship meals, and his mom went out of her way to make me food that was vegan. This poem is about them:

don't Love Me

Once,
when
i was
25,

i thought
i fell
in love

with
a boy.

BUT
I **didn't**.

I loved
how he
loved me.

--

++++
[and his
family]
was [were]

"cat
scavenging
my used
tampons
from the
bathroom
garbage-

-kill
them

all over
their house-

-and then
clean
them up,"

in love
with me.

One time he took me to the live orchestra of all
the "Final Fantasy" franchise music, downtown
Chicago. The space itself made me feel
incredibly self-conscious. And I have never
played Final Fantasy because I never owned
Playstations beyond a PlayStation one (the
controller is ick). The experience was undeniably
beautiful. We saw his ex and her parents, there,
and I was jealous. He loved me so much. More
than anyone ever had, and I loved how he loved
me more than I loved him. It hurt me so much to
learn that. But I stayed with him for months
anyway. I pretended that wasn't the case.
Because I didn't want to hurt him. He was the
first person to ever treat me like I deserved to be
treated, and I thought I couldn't lose him. Even if
it meant I would be with him for the rest of my
life, ignoring the fact that I wasn't particularly
attracted to him, and I'm queer.

Around this time, I actually finally applied to
enroll in the communication master's program I'd

taken classes in. I wrote application type letters that I had absolutely no idea how to write. So, I just told my story and what I'd survived. I had letters of recommendation from a few professors I had the last couple years who were kind enough to ignore the rest of my 2.6 GPA transcripts and take me on merit from only the years of my 4.0 GPA, specifically in communication coursework.

I was in my "incredible poet but hoarded house" boyfriend's room, sitting on his mattress on the floor (the rest of the floor, was a disaster zone), watching anime on his Crunchyroll, when I got the call hiring me for my very first teaching assistantship, starting my masters as an instructor of record. The same professor who encouraged me to apply called to award me that assistantship.

The entire first year that I taught public speaking, I had to face my fears about public speaking. As a couple, the way that he helped me do this was every Saturday night we would go to the same hole-in-the wall bar (that was in the same working-class town I lived in before I moved away from my PhD). There, I'd drink whiskey, cigarette smoke littered the air, and we'd sing our hearts out at karaoke. The DJ was an older coworker from the sexist owner's game shop. He'd picked this gig up on the side. For months, I sang the same songs over and over and over and over again, facing my biggest fear, and learning to feel comfortable in my own skin and voice.

I remember, most Saturday nights, there was also an older couple who would show up there too. The husband, I heard, developed dementia, and he loved to sing. His wife would bring him to the bar, so that he could still serenade her in public. At first, I didn't understand what exactly was happening. But once I learned, and ever since I saw them, it would absolutely break my fucking heart. It made me so full of emotion, I could barely contain it. And, one night, I couldn't contain it. For some reason, empty guy was there. I went out the back of the bar to cry my f'ing eyes out.

Empty guy ended up following me out, or somehow he got there. I told him why I was crying, and, of course, he gaslit me about it as if I had no reason to emotionally react to such a tragic romantic dynamic. As if he could possibly know what love is. I knew he could never understand what I felt like because he acted so fucking empty. So, I cried for him too, as he gaslit me for my autistic hyper-empathy. In the same breath, he wanted me to come back to him. He wanted me to sit in his house, and be nothing next to him. Because it made him feel like someone to hurt me.

I went back inside, distraught, and told my then boyfriend. He went to talk to empty guy outside. Afterward, my neurodivergent family guy boyfriend told me that he leveled with empty guy by saying " if you can love bird better than I can, by all means, be with them." That pitch spoke for itself. I never heard empty's answer, but I didn't need to. His not being there was answer enough.

I ended up, eventually, moving in with neurodivergent family guy. Our living arrangement worked for a little bit. (***But remember***, I didn't know I was autistic). I moved my full sized bed into our apartment, now full of almost all - just - my belongings. He helped me translate Japanese and Chinese websites to buy a kotatsu, after I learned they existed. I had sold my Xbox 360 for gas money after GTA V online stopped working, about a year prior, and I really missed playing video games because I had basically my entire life. So, he encouraged me to build a gaming PC, that then I built one myself off of YouTube videos (paid for using student loans). He had gotten a pretty good job in the corporate of a parking company and was making significantly more money than me. In his mind that meant that I should be doing all of our housework. He made it very clear. The real downfall of our relationship is that I am an autist who requires clean surroundings to function. And he required exactly the opposite. We stopped having sex. I tried to teach him once how to fold towels "the right way" and that went as disastrously as it sounds.

Around this time, I had my very first student I learned could not read. I learned that he had been passed through the K-12 education system his entire life, and never learned to read. And now he was in my class. He most likely had undiagnosed dyslexia. And his advisor reached out to me to ask about how he was doing. She explained to me the whole situation. He was failing basically all of his classes. Because, obviously, college classes require you to read at a college level. I remember sitting in this advisor's office, across her desk, and for the first time learning just how exploitative the corporatized education structure truly is. I became so full of rage that this sweet well-meaning boy could have been passed through Chicago public schools, and PUC had taken thousands of dollars from him to be here anyway, for nothing. I knew he loved to draw comics. But he was not properly prepared to be in class. He showed up to my class every day, anyway. It broke my fucking heart. It was the semester I learned so many people around me are being historically and intentionally failed. He grew up in a well-known socioeconomically and racially disenfranchised area. It was obviously not his lack of desire to learn. He was failed by a system that cares more about profit then people. And I knew he wasn't the only one living those failures.

On a differently tragic and concerning day not too long after this happened, one day in our small apartment bathroom, my vision went yellow and I fell to the floor. I didn't go to the doctor. (I have had heart palpitations at many random times throughout my twenties and also ignore them.)

Then (I don't know if it was before or after that), one day while a group of students were presenting a group speech on the movie Saving Private Ryan, and I sat there grading them, I started getting incredibly sweaty. I didn't know what was wrong, but I knew something bad was about to happen. I also got increasingly nauseous. More spit started developing in my mouth. And it occurred to me that I needed to get up because I was soon about to throw up, profusely.

I stood up suddenly in the middle of my student's group speech on a fictional military propaganda film and said, "I need a minute". But, as soon as I stood up, my vision turned to a wave of yellow, like a curtain closing top to bottom, and then my vision went to complete and total black. I stumbled into another desk in front of me. For a second, I considered that I might be blind for the rest of my life, and somewhat came to terms with it. My students had no idea what to do. But I loved this class, and they were very kind. I don't remember what I said next, but I did get out the door, grabbing the garbage can, and threw up profusely outside the classroom.

The next thing I remember was going back in after and saying, "Human bodies, am I right?"

My relatively small class burst into laughter at the absurdity of it all, and I felt comedically redeemed, albeit scared. I told them we were going to push the rest of the speeches until next class, and they all completely understood. One of them grabbed me a little paper cup of cold water. Most of them walked with me out of the class and did their best to sympathize with me.

As the universe would have it, after that class, I decided to sit in a lounge chair in the hallway (of a campus building that later was fully gutted because, turns out, the decrepit ass fucking walls were entirely full of dangerous mold) my student who I just learned couldn't read from my other class, happened to walk by and see me. I'll never forget that he asked me what was wrong, and I said I didn't feel well, and he just said to me, "You should go home and take care of yourself."

I remember sitting there after he walked away saying something, so obvious, thinking to myself "I am in my masters, teaching college classes, and I can't do basic things to take care of myself".

I had no idea what was medically wrong with me. And I didn't go to the doctor to find out. It might've been, I barely drank water. It might have been, I was allergic to the overly dry peanut butter bread I had for breakfast. (It might have been I have POTS/EDS, or the countless other newly documented increasingly long list of comorbidities that autists frequently also develop.)

Not too long after that mysterious medical event causing a disruption in my classroom, the pressure from never being able to be alone because I lived with neurodivergent family guy became too much. We would get into fights, and I would go under my comforter backwards in the dark and need to be alone. He would ask me some questions, but I couldn't get myself to physically speak. And I didn't understand why. I didn't understand why I just couldn't speak to answer his questions. And it made me feel terrible about myself. He was the one person I had disclosed some of my sexual violence to, and he was understanding. But I couldn't stand sharing my full-size bed with him, and never being able to unmask. No matter how much he loved me. I couldn't unmask my autism completely around him. (And to this day, I don't understand why.)

So, I started texting newspaper friend about it. One thing I've always absolutely adored about newspaper friend (other than most everything about him), is that as someone born and raised into "digital nomad"-ness since my early life, I have had to, impossibly, become hyper attuned to the absence of nonverbals, existing in text-only communications. And learning that, often times, has meant that I fell on my fucking face by sending way too much text. But when I talk with him, he's never once made me feel like I've sent too much text. And that is a very rare, special thing, after a lifetime of basically always being made to feel like too much for the people around me.

Anyway, I told newspaper friend that I knew I needed to leave neurodivergent family guy because I couldn't even stand sleeping in the same bed with him anymore. (At the time, I didn't know I was autistic, so I must have just sounded like a terrible person.) One night, I finally had a meltdown about it, and he became afraid of me during it. He got scared because his dad, and he called 911. His name was on the lease, not mine. Cops did nothing besides tell me "his name is on the lease and he can kick you out, so, you're gonna need to come to some sort of agreement".

They left, and we agreed to break up, and he moved all of his stuff into the office. And because my bed was in our bedroom, I also moved my stuff from the office, into there. It sucks to say this, but once I moved everything and had my own space, I had an immediate sense of relief. I didn't know how to describe it at the time, and he probably was so confused and heartbroken.

To make matters worse empty guy started texting me, and a part of me missed being at his house, because there, I could just turn off my fucking brain, and act dead. I didn't have to be anything or anyone when I was at his house. So, one day after that, I went back. One thing led to another, and we messed around. Our chemistry was still there, and, yes, I felt absolutely terrible about it.

Even though I had already ended things with neurodivergent family guy, not very long ago, I also knew that this was going to break his fucking heart. (I know objectively this was a terrible thing to do. This was not the way to handle it. This was an absolute piece of shit way to do it. At least, I know what it felt like to be cheated on a few years after my ex-boyfriend r***d me, cheated on me, and then I lost $200 in gifts to him. I don't know what part of my mind thought that this was the way to end things, but it happened. This was absolutely me being *the bad guy*.)

Shortly after this I told neurodivergent family guy what had happened with empty guy and me. Then, I moved out of our apartment and back in with my parents. After I moved out, he had basically no furniture, and he couldn't afford the rent on his own, so he did too. Understandably, the guy friend who supported me through trying to end the fuckin fiasco with empty guy (and was also friends with neurodivergent family guy) could not believe what I'd done and told me.

Only a few visits later to empty guy's house, it was already clear to me that I was such a different person compared to who I was when we first met, that we couldn't stand being around each other anymore. Because of what I learned, we had become like oil and water. The last night I ever went over to his parent's house, we got into our first and last fight that turned physical.

I don't remember what happened before this, but I do remember that I tried to playfully put my arms around him from behind for some reason, but he thought I was attacking him. I had long nails at the time, that I cut into points. So, one of my nails scratched across the front of his neck, leaving a line, since in one fell swoop, he lifted me over his shoulder, and body slammed me onto my back to his floor (covered in all sorts of shit). So, I got up, left, and never came back.

Not too long after, against my better judgement, I went to the game shop (that I'd quit earlier) to meet the "disappointed in me for hurting neurodivergent family guy" friend. Oddly, empty guy showed up, and I saw that he had a scratch from my nail across his neck. It most likely bled.

At the time, I also had some hidden bruises on random parts of my body from him: legs, torso. And I gotta be honest. I had felt a little vindicated seeing that, after all the pain he'd caused me.

If me feeling like that makes me "the bad guy" after how he treated me: That's fine ¯_(ツ)_/¯

Well, Actually, I Would Rather Be "The Bad Guy"

Right at the end of my bachelor's program, my sister had already had her first child with her second husband. A guy she best in high school. Their first kid was assigned female at birth, and they've raised her to be a girl. As stated in chapter one, my sister and I are complete and total opposites. She is Gen X, and I am a late millennial. We were born and raised in two completely different worlds. She's always been more religious than me, even though one time when she was growing up, a teacher at her Catholic school had the nerve to call her "stupid" and she was then transferred out into public school. (She didn't deserve that shit, no matter what she's done since.)

As a PDA profile autist, one of my trademark things is that I love to research as much as I possibly can about a specific topic, and then share that information with people I think it could help. Since I had just taken all those courses about cisheterosexism, and my sister now had a daughter she was raising, I thought she might like to know about some of it. I was learning a lot about systemic oppressions for the very first time in my entire life, and I didn't want anyone in my life to experience them unknowingly like I had. I had a belief that information could help others be more well-informed. Because it's certainly helped me. So, I sent my sister a long email sharing information with her about historical sexisms. I shared with her my concerns, as kindly as I could, about her raising her daughter to be only a wife and mother, in a world that, for the first time, was actually allowing AFABs to be anyone else. I had the best intentions in sending that information because I thought that she would take it the right way and she'd like to know.

But my sister did not take it the right way, and did not like to know. She became incredibly defensive and accused me of attempting to backseat parent her children. She said that she feels liberated in her lifestyle with her husband as the head of the house, and that she'll raise her children however she wants. On one hand, I fully got that. I had learned about separatist feminisms, popular in conservative movements. I was like, sure, obviously live your life however you want. But I was not yet at a point in my life where I knew I was autistic. I didn't understand why she was receiving my well-intentioned information sharing as a threat. I also realistically, wasn't well-informed enough to understand the nuances. My biggest concern is that her daughter could experience levels of violence that I have because if she is not taught to protect herself, something really bad could happen. I knew what it was like to have many really bad things happen to myself. And I didn't want anything like that to happen to any of my nieces.

One of the final straws before our decade long falling out was I attended my niece's birthday party, when she was probably about three or four years old, and I saw that she was getting picked on by other homeschooled little boys who I had to tell, forcefully, not to push my niece down. I didn't have the information that I have now at the time to explain why I was so scared for her.

My lifetime of autistic shame that I have internalized, and the traumas I'd lived were so far suppressed I couldn't have articulated or responded then in a way that would've explained why my concerns existed. So instead, I tried to bite my tongue, and grew increasingly Bern'd out. Soon, I couldn't be around her family anymore without just completely having a meltdown and snapping because of the constant expectation on me to conform to cisheteronormativity, knowing the violences that those norms cause, and being treated like "the bad guy" for saying anything.

My Not So Sweet-2016

One day after the first year of my master's, I attended a screening of a documentary about targeted restriction on abortion provider (TRAP) laws. After the screening, there was a question and answer period in which I asked how I can get involved with the cause, as someone who studies rhetoric. After that discussion was over, a Democratic candidate came up to me and said they wanted me to be their campaign manager. I was also propositioned by a Planned Parenthood sex educator, who needed her replacement. So, at the time, I thought I was being presented with two incredible opportunities that'd allow me to get involved in work that was important to me.

I struggled to decide for a little while and then I chose to reach out to the Democratic candidate to learn more about her proposition. We talked, and she said that everything for her campaign needed go through the Indiana Dem. House caucus, and that someone else was already chosen for her. But she said she wanted me to be on her team. She asked what other sorts of skills I had, and I said, "Well I know how to do social media management". And she said, "OK, great, if you could create me a Facebook page, you could be my Internet officer". I agreed. Then, one day she called and invited me to go to a two-day training in Indianapolis, last minute. I drove two hours there and spent the day. I was under the impression that I wasn't gonna be her campaign manager at the time because she told me that. I became confused because the vast majority of other people that were there were campaign managers, so I was thinking, "What the hell am I doing here?"

Before I went for the second day, she'd given me another random abrupt call, as she often did moving forward, saying her other campaign manager dropped out, and she wanted me to take over. She'd already been a state representative for her district before. And she had a good chance of winning again. She was from East Chicago, in the Harbor. But, nowadays, she was a lawyer and bragged about how she shouldn't wear her Rolex to union meetings. Her mom was a teacher, and so she spoke about the importance of education. And the rest was all Democratic Party approved language, that I got from their website. As time went on, she became increasingly rude. She didn't let me have an office, which she could've easily paid $100 for so I could get a key to the local politicians official building she sent me to. Instead, she put me in an uncomfortable position where she just never paid them, so I could get a key (but I only learned that much later).

The people running the well-established politician's office I did not have a key to thought very highly of themselves and made it abundantly clear. They were "politicians in the making". A Corporate Couple, very sure one of them would run for office, shortly thereafter. I learned a lot about politics from that experience. I learned that almost all politics involves making favors for one another. Doing fundraisers. Asking for volunteers to do things for you. Making endless phone calls. And then, of course, serving as your rude ass candidate's fucking therapist. My candidate was notorious for being incredibly mean. She treated her previous campaign managers terribly, and I was no different. I did basically everything for her, that she let me do. I had absolutely no experience doing it. And yet based off of the data that I had, recording our progress of canvassing and phone banking, I was the most successful campaign manager on the team.

I would go out basically every single day in the hot summer sun and canvas almost entirely alone unless I got volunteers that day to go around different neighborhoods and knock on door after door after door, trying to talk to random strangers, and making her sound like a great person. I had so many citizens go around telling me "you should be running". They asked me if I was the candidate. They told me "if I wasn't I should be". Door after door after door, I heard citizens who said they'd lost faith in the two-party system. For at least the last year and my coursework, I had been learning and feeling the exact same way. Before getting paid enough by the Democratic Party to be their lacky that summer, I was learning about how neoliberalism is a philosophic and economic model that started in the 70s. I learned about media monopolization by the neoliberal transnational capitalist class, of which my master's mentor was an expert in. I learned about how systems will do everything they possibly can to exploit a populous into believing in reformism.

Which is to say, I knew better when the Democratic state representation offered me this fucking job than to work for the late stage capitalist Democratic Party. But I could barely afford to live, because I was living off of credit, a completely unlivable stipend to teach one or two college classes, and student loans. They offered me two grand a month and I took it. Because I needed to survive. And I thought that it might actually allow me to speak truth to power and talk to people.

In certain senses, it did do that for me. My experience working for the Democratic Party Indiana House Caucus did give me a golden opportunity I wouldn't have otherwise had to learn how the system works from the inside. I spoke with numerous unions, representatives, and lifelong teachers, steelworkers, etc. in the Region. I learned that many in these professions can't afford to live anymore. I learned more of them than ever before were choosing to retire because of things like state-profitable standardized tests, and union leaders not advocating in the way that they're supposed to because of incrementalism. Because of the way that corporate culture mediates humans to sway others, and pulls people under its wing, caving in ways that hurt workers' rights.

I talked to citizens who are "anti-union" because I learned that they had misplaced blame on union workers and were heavily propagandized to think unions were *bad* instead of billionaires.

In 2016, I also learned that Pokémon Go is really fucking fun. Because that was the summer that Pokémon Go came out. And what better time to work for the soul sucking late-stage capitalist neoliberal Democratic Party, canvassing door-to-door, than when Pokémon Go was in its prime?

I don't know if readers remember how miraculous the year before Trump got elected really was. That summer before the 2016 election was a very special time to be alive. I took full advantage of that. Yes, I was working 80-hour weeks. But I was also walking around a local park that was next to the subdivision I grew up in, with folks who I'd barely known growing up, and new eyes.

In the golden age of Pokémon Go everyone in your general vicinity was either your best friend or your greatest enemy. It was a time that made the physical world feel absolutely augmented-reality magical. That silly little fucking app got me to exercise unlike anything ever had before. It also made me sit in my car at an obscure, but precise location, and proceed to catch fake lil guys.

Speaking of fake little guys, around this time, I got a crush on someone from seeing them walking around the park who was a year ahead of me in high school. He was always kinda goofy, and I never really knew much about him. For some reason he seemed more attractive that year. I've always had a thing for goofy little fucking guys, that are rather vulgar. And he fit the bill. He made me rather nervous. And everyone knows what I do when I'm nervous in public; I drink. And, boy, did I drink around this man. He was one of the only people that I ever used Snapchat with. Our streak was very impressive, if I do say so myself. He was very sexual and very fun, and I really enjoyed that about him. I, however, was still an unrealized autistic person.

One night we went out to a local brewery, in a neighboring town just over the border into Illinois that I, unfortunately, knew empty guy also frequented, and the possibility that he might walk in during our date made me unendingly anxious. So much so that, despite this being a local brewery for craft beer, I had a number of very strong drinks. We talked and had fun, as usual. The night got later, and I got drunker. We went to another bar. And I got drunker still. This made me a little bit more comfortable around him, but also a lot more unable to control my body. One of the last things I remember is being at the bar and sitting next to him, me getting a little handsy with him.

The next morning, I woke up laying on his bed at his parent's house. I'd never been in his room before, and I realized I had dried throw up on my tiny shirt. I asked him what the fuck happened? And he said, I got so incredibly drunk that we got back to his house, and I got so violently ill in the bathroom, that as it happened, his dogs wouldn't stop barking at me, profusely throwing up in the bathroom. It woke up his entire family. I had no recollection of even leaving the bar. He drove me back to my car, and I felt absolutely terrible. Both because of what had happened (his poor trying to sleep family in the middle of the night), and my head was also fucking killing me.

The thing about being autistic and hung over is that if you are not autistic and think you've had a bad hangover – I'm sorry, no, you haven't. I will never forget the taste in my mouth from nearly my entire twenties, after numerous nights of heavy drinking into sickness and black out. The feeling that happens in my head is like my brain turns into an actual tundra. I have memories of when I was young, before other houses were built in my subdivision of patches of dried earth.

The kind that breaks apart and cracks, almost like a mosaic. That's exactly how my brain feels, after a terribly bad hangover. I feel swear I feel the absence of liquid inside my brain folds. Like as if my body and mind were trying to say, "We are an entire ecosystem. Please stop killing us."

The only thing that would work around this time was drinking entire large cans of coconut water and/or visiting a little vegan café that was in the town that my mom grew up in. I would go there, quite frequently, because the food was fucking bomb, even though it was incredibly overpriced. They have this drink there that was made from sprouted beans, and then they would put it in some lemonade, and that shit filled in my brain cracks. So, that morning I knew that I needed to go there and partake in watering my brain folds. I went, and thank fucking Goddess, it worked.

The remainder of that summer, I kept working as this rude ass Democrat's campaign manager, canvassing door-to-door. Because it was a hot summer I'd often times wear summer dresses. I have never had very big breasts, and so a lot of the time, I just don't wear a bra because it's my fucking body and it's my fucking choice if and when I *ever* wear a bra, no matter where I work.

One day I received an email sent to "my entire team", talking about dressing "professional", and saying a lot of bullshit to only say "wear a bra". I was at a veteran's organization from my candidate. She couldn't attend that day. As she often couldn't. So I was a stand in for her presence. As if my being there was her by proxy. In politic eyes, I was nothing but her extension.

I emailed my direct superior back at the Indiana Democratic House Caucus asking if bra email was about me. She didn't give me a real answer. I am autistic, but even I knew what that meant.

The semester started, and I got a call from the Indiana Democratic House Caucus telling me that if I didn't give up my teaching assistantship, I would be fired. I told them that I would only be teaching part-time and I was told at the beginning of the job that my doing both would be just fine. They told me they changed their minds. Then, I gave up my teaching assistantship, gathered volunteers for them for a week during the first busiest week of the semester, and then they fired me, anyway. So, in one fell swoop, the Democratic Party destroyed both of my only incomes.

I was completely distraught by this, for many days, until I realized that I knew better than to trust the fucking Democratic Party. They did exactly what I knew they do, to people that have more radical beliefs. And I apparently thought that I was not going to experience that same treatment.

The next day, my direct superior asked for my candidate's Facebook username and password (that I created), and I told her, "Sorry, I made that before y'all hired me on. That isn't a part of my campaign management". Fuck that candidate and fuck the corporate ass Democratic party.

It's Wackadoodle Time

I was living with my parents again, and campaign managing was the one job I ever had they actually expressed that they were proud of me for. Shortly after I was fired, it became impossible to live at their house again. I didn't know how I was going to do it, but I needed to move out.

So, I did what I had to. I found a tiny apartment across the street from my favorite coffee shop in my favorite town, and I signed a lease, with no job. I told myself: I will find a job, it will be fine.

And, the next day, I did find a job, working at a call center for newspapers all around the country, and it was fine. Until it Wasn't Fine. I don't know if readers have ever worked at a call center before, but that shit fucking blows. It's bad enough for anyone, let alone a PDA autist that had half of a master's degree, and a critical specialization in the exact industry the call-center was for. An industry that was slowly being replaced by digital medias, yet continuing to struggle to pretend like it wasn't. I worked in the department people called to cancel their newspapers. So, I knew -- full well -- just how much the average citizen wanted to cancel their fucking papers. It was my job to know about it. It was also my job to be micromanaged and constantly be on the phone, from the second I clocked in, to the second they data colonized my clocking out.

Otherwise, the job was easy enough, even though their main software was incredibly outdated. There was a lot of multitasking, and a lot of emotional labor, that at the end of the day, I'm really just not well suited for. I have never been able to successfully control my tone. And I often come across as "far too direct" for the average non-autistic person. But this was a job and I needed one.

Right around the time I inevitably began to not be able to physically, emotionally, or mentally handle working that job anymore, the owner of the vegan café asked me if I would like to work there part-time for just free food and tips. I said Sure. Because I did like vegan food and cash.

It was around that time that a Gen X man, in his forties, came into the café, who I'd seen before, but I never really knew anything about. I knew he was a poet. I knew that some of my friends from the coffee shop knew him. It didn't occur to me, yet that I'd heard his poems that he would record and place CDs of around town, sharing intimate parts of his life, like it was no big deal.

After losing my teaching assistantship which I loved and then proceeding to be exploited for shit pay and to be emotionally beaten down by strangers who hated their newspaper, and took it out on me (the faceless cog who represented said newspaper I worked for, since corporations use us workers as punching bags) I drank, heavily. I had just worked 80-hour weeks all summer, so I had plenty of expendable income to do so. And there was also a new Beercade in town. So, what better time to play Sunset Riders and get absolutely sloshed on an 8% beer and fancy cocktails?

Boy, did I love to do that. When I say that it's an absolute miracle that I completed my masters, while doing any readings, and drinking as heavily as I was. I mean, I should absolutely be dead.

One night I was at said favorite local beercade, and someone down the bar, I then didn't really recognize, bought me a drink. I was already sloshed at the time, and the beer was over 10%, so instead of drinking it, I walked back to my little apartment, since I wasn't trying to die that night.

Later, I learned he that same shallow Gen X guy, rather chauvinistic, who liked Morrissey far too much. I ended up getting to know this guy far better than I ever expected. And although he cared too much about what other people thought about him (and I), and he drink far too much (just like I did, almost every day, then), he inspired me to write poetry. I can't thank him enough for that.

As time went on, I spent far too many days of the week at the bar/bowling alley next to my apartment, and this Beercade. It would've been easier if basically, every single night, every person I'd ever known wasn't there. But they were, and so I was too. Eventually, I ran into another guy who was actually friends with that other guy I knew who was also a year ahead of me in high school. In fact, him and the guy who's house I got incredibly booze-sick at and made his family dogs bark late into the night used to be really good friends when we were all younger.

This new guy was one of the funniest motherfuckers I've ever met in my entire life, and I knew it as soon as I'd met him the first time. He also had a face and body chiseled like an actual statue. Plus, he was brilliant, thoughtful, and we just really got along. But like many of us, this guy also didn't have a very healthy home life. Funny guy and I would smoke and hang out in his car and talk for hours and hours and hours. I really enjoyed his company. He saw so much potential in me and the person I was becoming then, despite all my flaws and unknowns, and I really saw it.

We were sitting at the Beercade bar the night 45 was elected president. We were both devastated for different, but historically parallel, identity-based legitimate reasons. We went out to the back of the bar and stood outside while he smoked, talking about how much more scary and hateful the world might become, than it already was. We didn't know then, but at the same time, we did.

A few weeks after the election, I was contacted by someone I hadn't heard from in a number of months through Facebook messenger. I met them while they worked for a parallel campaign to the one that I managed, and they told me that, "they wanted me to know, their direct superior said that I was fired for not wearing a bra. They didn't think that was right." But, apparently, they thought that it was "right" enough to not tell me until after the election and they got paid.

(To learn significantly more about this entire fiasco, read my "Requirement Politics" article.)

Soon after, funny guy and I went out, and I drank far too much (as I often did). But, he said that I acted like an entirely different person. I thought "fine, yes, I know that black out drunk people act different". Then he told me one of his parents actually had a drinking problem, and, so, he couldn't be with me if there was any chance I would act like that ever again. And, so obviously, since there was a chance I might, we were donezo. (Suspiciously, though, when I was drunk, and apparently too drunk for him, I was also still sober enough in his mind to have sex with anyway.)

He bared the news to me in text, amicably. I understood, but it did break my absolute fucking heart then. It hurt unlike anything ever hurt me because I thought it was totally my fault. At least at the time, I thought I was just *the bad guy* who couldn't control their drinking for no reason. (I didn't understand yet that the main reason I drank so heavily was because it was a socially acceptable, heavily commodified way, that I, an undiagnosed autist, became accustomed to existing in public. So, here, I guess we might say that I was both *the bad guy* and "the bad guy".

Eventually, I went to my mentor and begged for my teaching assistantship back because I needed to regain my sense of identity. Thankfully, he obliged, and I was able to teach again the next, final year of my masters. I continued to drink heavily and began to flirt and casually make out with a stoner guy who worked at the beercade (beer + arcade). He played retro video games, smoked, and drew. He was a very good kisser, got many kissers, and I had a lot of fun with him.

You Had A Rough 2017? Me Too

The semester before the end of my Masters, it occurred to me that because of my having taken a number of graduate courses, while also completing my minor in communication, I'd have enough credits to graduate a semester sooner than I thought. I was shook. Other teaching assistants in my office asked me if I was going to apply to PhD programs, which to my anxious and terrified surprise, all had deadlines that, if I wanted to do so, were in one month. Obviously, I fucking panicked. If I didn't do that, I would've had to wait a full year. And in the meantime, my student loans would've started to kick in, cause I would've been over six months. So, I had absolutely no choice. I had to pursue a PhD. And, honestly, I wanted to. This work was the one thing in my life that gave me a sense of meaning, and I wasn't ready to give it up without a fight.

The year was 2017. The #metoo campaign, just happened. I was a 27-year-old lifelong deeply suppressed autistic sexual violence survivor, who drink far too much for reasons I didn't actually fully comprehend, and only just began writing poetry, thanks to my muse at the time, and was now deeply in need of letter writers to apply to PhD programs within a single short months' time.

Thankfully, many of my letter writers from my master's app. were willing to write another letter for this. But it's honestly a miracle it even worked at all. I applied to around four or five allegedly "prestigious" schools I don't even remember. I prepped for the GRE in about two weeks and took it as an unrealized autist (who enjoyed the sound canceling headphones they allowed us to wear during it, a little too much). I took the GRE, B12 deficient, and with a cold. And I scored totally average on it, as I always did on standardized tests, my entire fucking life.

I paid multiple too expensive PhD program application fees and submitted my ambitious applications to the handful of "out of my league" schools, and one school that happened to reach out to my department because they had had successful hardworking students come from there, previously. The uni. department who reached out to ours was Bowling Green State University.

A brilliant friend of mine from my masters was also applying to PhD programs at the time, and they taught me the ropes. I, anxiously, watched the PhD acceptance websites. I got a number of rejection letters, first, from the "too good for me" programs. Then to my surprise, while I attended a conference in Milwaukee with colleagues, my acceptance letter and teaching associateship offer for the BGSU Media & Communication program. I couldn't believe it worked. It looked like money I might be able to live on (I was absolutely wrong about that).

The rest of that last semester of my masters and living in the Region was a complete anxious, drunken blur. I was aware, it didn't fucking matter what I got on grades in that final semester because I was already accepted into a PhD program. The only thing standing between me and getting a master's degree was writing a "convention ready" paper about the #metoo campaign.

I wrote around 74 pages in a day, that was, in hindsight, an almost completely unintelligible infodump. But very comprehensive, as is my style whenever I write a first draft of anything.

I completed my required comprehensive exams. My mentor gave me a C on that first draft of my #MeToo campaign project paper (it became a book chapter). I officially had a master's degree.

That summer before my PhD was absolutely surreal. I basically stop drinking, started exercising a lot, and did yoga, basically, every day. For the first time in my life, I felt like I might become someone. No one in my family assigned female at birth ever earned a PhD. They couldn't of, the world didn't allow them to during their lifetimes. Even though I basically couldn't talk to almost all of my family, this was a big deal for our bloodline, and I felt an enormous responsibility still.

On one drunken, probably weekday, night around then, I came across a YouTube video. This YouTube video was about "female" autism. At the time, I knew so little about autism, that most of my life I would, quite literally, confuse Down Syndrome and autism, as if they're the same thing. I thought autism was just Rain Man (Since I was taught zero disability knowledge and endless ableisms, like most of the U.S. populace, to this day). Then, I bawled my fucking eyes out because – somehow -- a woman in a YouTube knew -- absolutely everything -- that I had kept hidden from both my actual self, and everyone else in my fucking life for 27 fucking years.

Which is to say, like most autistic people who have realized that they are a member of one of the countless lost generations of autistic people, because of the failed criteria of autism, I didn't just "self-diagnose myself off of a single TikTok that said, I like to use a big spoon". I did so after hiding it for years, meeting basically all of the criteria. My autism only became more prominent after I processed my lifetime of traumas, and then

I spent years doing research about why the lost generations were failed, in the first place, and began revisiting my entire life. My entire life that I have felt absolutely terrible about myself, and endured mistreatment from most everyone.

A life, I treated myself, and others, badly in because I was inevitably fucking miserable from it.

This was an incredibly important summer for me in my self-realized neuroqueer journey. Because even though it felt like a void, before I left everyone and everything I ever knew before, it also brought me back to my body for the first time in a very long time. In the beginning, I was still drinking, and occasionally, would show up on Saturday mornings to yoga, hung over as fuck, and to the most intense practice I had ever experienced in my whole fucking life. But I'd found the best yoga instructor I could've possibly wished for. She taught me how to push myself in a way I didn't know was physically possible and to gain strength to endure difficult poses.

This mental/physical practice tested me both mentally and physically in a way I never endured before. And alongside some of the coolest people I've ever met, I learned how to do headstands. I remember the first time she had us do headstands, and I was so scared. But it was at the end of the session, so I was also *Flying*. She had one of those inversion seats. (You know the ones.) They have the handles, and then you put your head through the hole, and there's cushions for your shoulders, so if you're terrified at the thought of inversions, it is definitely the seat for you.

Anyway, I did it and I remember having an unforgettable feeling that my X and Y axis were now reversed. My mind could barely handle the flip. I've always had a strange relationship with core strength. I have a very strange posture. Yet, I never cared enough to adjust it. Even though I know that the standard is you're supposed to stand upright. This was around the time I learned what an "anterior pelvic tilt" is. I learned that I definitely had that shit. Which, for anyone who doesn't know, that makes doing inversions, like headstands, very difficult.

You really need to have hella good alignment, core strength, and general grounding to be able to properly do any inversion. Once I could, I would do headstands everywhere after that. Anyone who saw my Instagram at the time can attest of that 😄 I became an upside down menace. For me, it physically made real the way that I always felt like I saw the world. From a dramatically difference. And it broke me out of the seriousness of the day, reminding me that I can play.

Since I'd long moved into the little apartment across the street from my favorite coffee shop in the Region (that some of the coolest people owned), one day, my mom and I went bowling at the alley next door. (I don't remember, but it might've been her birthday. I've never been good at remembering anyone's birthday). Either way we went to that one in this town she grew up in. The thing about my mom was she used to bowl *really well* when she was younger. She won trophies, and wanted to become a professional, until she hurt her hand. She was left-handed too.

Another thing I forgot to mention about her is that at some point in her life, she became a yoga instructor. But she never taught classes besides for a few people here and there, in the basement of that first house (I'd spent most of my childhood in). She wanted me to care about Yoga then. But I could never care about Yoga. And, around the time that she learned that I was finally into yoga, she had advanced lung cancer. So, she bought me a class subscription at a yoga studio.

It's Time to Fly the Coop, Bern'd Out Lil' bird

Another thing about my mom, and really both my parents, is that she was raised to believe that Black people are "criminals" and that pointing that out "isn't racist" (So more of the same old shit I've heard, basically my whole life, first played into myself as a young naïve autistic child, and then eventually have worked to unlearn alongside every other discrimination brought to my awareness). So, four days before I moved to PhD-land, my aunt and uncle on my mom's side and my parents and I went to "lunch" at a Mexican restaurant. I haven't talked about them because they weren't relevant but *are* — absolutely terrible. My uncle was a cop for most of his life, but most of my life, he's been just a conspiracy theorist. He always sat at our bar during holidays and would be like muttering himself that the communists were going to make a currency or whatever.

He's the dad of my creepy older cousin, who had built our first house in Munster. And they all used to be a part of this cult called the Westborough Baptist Church. For anyone who doesn't know, it is now notorious around the Region for having these blue buses that they'd drive around, and, for being p3dos. So, there's a lot to unpack there. But this is my memoir, not theirs.

Anyway, the five of us, that day, all met at this fucking Mexican restaurant that my mom and aunt almost always went to, to drink margaritas, despite both of their long-internalized racisms.

I ordered a coffee because I am vegan, and I couldn't eat anything there. I decided not to say anything about it because I didn't want to center myself even though we were also there in part as a tiny gesture of going away, and my being the first AFAB person in our line, pursuing a PhD.

Anyway, not too long after I'd gotten my shitty, but loveable, basically, diner coffee, they started saying racist shit inside this Mexican restaurant. My creepy older cousin's son apparently started smoking weed, and they were blaming it on his new Black friend "being a bad influence." So, I asked them basic questions, and they couldn't fucking hang. The next thing I knew I was being screamed at, in the middle of that Mexican restaurant, just for asking family members (my mom and dad, sitting in silence supporting them) -- my horrific aunt and uncle -- why they thought Fox News is a credible source when it is -- matter-of-factly – just billionaire owned propaganda.

Near the end, before he stormed out for basically no reason, my creepy older cousin mocked me for not shaving my legs, as if my body hair has any bearing on my ability to teach college (a position I had succeeded at for at least 2 years already, but they wouldn't know that because we never talked). After they were done screaming dog whistles in the middle of a fucking Mexican restaurant, I said, "Thanks for the invite. Can't imagine why I don't come around more often!" and I stood up, gave them a peace sign, and walked out. I haven't spoken to those fuckers since.

Anyway, four short days of packing later, thanks to my mom gifting me $2000 (of her corporate lung cancer silence blood money) for my long distance move, I moved to Ohio to pursue dreams.

The morning I left, I still felt absolutely and completely betrayed by my parents and my bigoted fucking aunt and uncle, but specifically, my parents for not speaking up for me when I was being publicly humiliated by my mom's racist fucking brother-in-law, and creepy fucking older cousin, who -- at the time by the way – to absolutely no one's surprise – was also wearing one of those -- absolutely foolish – t-shirts that said something like "Own the Libs" with an American flag on it.

So that's the story of how basically every single member of my entire family had treated me as "the bad guy" and why my aunt, uncle, and creepy older cousin are, and can stay, "dead" to me.

O-"hi"-oh

Then, I moved my entire life to a place I knew no one, and for a few months lived in my rented house, waiting for my very first PhD semester to begin (while doing exactly the right amount of headstands, wearing a questionable amount of clothing, and posting it all onto my Instagram).

The coursework years of my PhD were an overworked blur. The first week, I met who would become my first PhD mentor. He reminded of myself for reasons I didn't understand. That same week, it became clear to me that unless I took every syllabus, and other responsibility in my life, and wrote all deadlines down into my agenda, for all semester, alongside placing visible post-it notes onto my desk in front of me (to see every single day), I was going to fucking drown in deadlines, and fail out of my PhD faster than anyone could call me *the bad guy* or "the bad guy".

So, that's exactly what I did. I micromanaged every single one of my days. I was too autistic to know that I was not in fact supposed to be reading every single word of every single assigned reading. So, in my very stereotypically literal interpretation of my assigned reading, I read it all. Therefore, to even begin managing to do so, I had zero life, besides sitting somewhere (our shared teaching assistantship office, or a nearby coffee shop) from 8 am until 10:30 pm, daily. I did what I needed to do, and to my surprise, I did do it -- on zero water and too much coffee. At the end of each semester during my two year-round coursework, I relearned how to live/breathe. My fight or flight was already triggered my entire fucking life by basic demands. I was used to it.

That first semester, my new mentor taught me all about what "media ecology" is, in a way that actually made me care about it. He also assigned readings that I absolutely loved, like John Durham Peter's book *Speaking Into the Air*. (Later, that following summer, whether due to the universe or the cult-like world of academia, I learned my master's mentor was Peter's advisee).

Online, I started noticing that there were leftists sharing memes that were actually raising everyday people's political consciousness, and so I wrote a paper about Leftbook (leftist + Facebook = Leftbook). My mentor edited it, I submitted it to my very first Media Ecology Association convention in Toronto. I won their Top Convention paper for it (while also within a few days' time of seeing Canada for the very first time at my first MEA, was also sexually harassed by "the last living man to have worked with Marshall McLuhan". It was a whirlwind. I wrote a letter to the MEA board and asked for something to be done. Due to the advocacy of my mentor, and another colleague I had just met, the board created the first Misconduct Committee. (My Leftbook paper then was published in a later issue of their journal and was my first article.)

By the time I had attended that, I had already submit a proposal to be on the very first "Gender and Media Ecology" panel at the National Communication Association convention. For those who are not affiliated with academia, that is the big U.S. conference of media & communication. My proposal there, presenting what later went on to become my dissertation, was later accepted.

Eventually, Trump threatened to kill TikTok, and so I finally joined the party. To be honest, it really fucking overstimulated me for about the first four days I was there. And I almost gave up on it because of how terribly "normal" the default algorithm was. But I scrolled, and the longer I scrolled the more it gave me really eerily "me" shit. Shit no one could've possibly known about my ass because of my lifetime of secrets. Shit that fit me and described "me "to me, as I actually knew that I was, and in a way no one else could've possibly known. That's when I stumbled into autistic TikTok. Because, after spending, Goddess knows how many hours on the app, its unique algorithm was miraculously able to identify me, despite my having hid, my entire fucking life.

At the time, how the TikTok algorithm could "know" all these things about me was completely unexplainable to me. And then, I started to remember I'd seen a YouTube video in 2017, before I started my PhD, and I bawled my fucking eyes out, knowing in that moment, unequivocally, that "I am autistic. And now, what the fuck do I do with that information? I'm about to start a PhD."

As I did research, I learned the TikTok user-base, which used to be primarily just Gen Z folks (younger people), exploded over early years of COVID-19, and was being seen as a legitimate digital space/subject for research because of it being the single most datafied platform to exist.

Which is to say, like most every lost autistic person who is alive right now, recently realizing that they are a member of one of the – many -- lost generations of autistic people (because of the failed criteria of autism), I didn't just "self-diagnose myself off of one TikTok that said, 'I like to use a big spoon'". I did so after hiding it for years, while meeting all of the criteria. Then, my traits only became more prominent after I processed my entire lifetime of trauma. And then, I spent years doing research about why our generations were failed in the first place, catalyzing a reprocessing of my life. My life where I felt -- absolutely terrible -- about myself, and treated myself, and sometimes others, badly since I was so – inevitably -- fucking miserable from that.

I suppressed the fact I met all the criteria. I didn't think about it the first two years of my PhD, while I continued being blatantly autistic, and then sought the second opinion of the therapist I was working with to process my lifetime of sexual violences (after I won the Top Convention paper at my very first MEA convention in 2019) -- who agreed, I met the autism criteria and was very upfront and explicit with me that, "because of how ableist this world is, I shouldn't get a formal Dx ,since it'd hurt me more than help me now". If you've seen the research from the last fifteen years and listen to the overwhelming accounts from autistic people who amend the failed diagnostics with experiential criteria, you know what autism actually is, and I am clearly autistic.

The fact of the matter is, most unrecognized autistics and non-autistics, alike, are/were both socialized to believe, speak about, and treat autists as less than human and "other" for most of human history. So, if they've known someone, under the impression that they "weren't autistic", it's threatening for you to expand your understandings of what autism has actually always been.

Non-autistics, or autists, with internalized ableism about other autistics (which is so incredibly common, and I am unpacking it too) often have developed extensive reasons as to why they grew to distain or hate autists for reasons they don't understand are *because of autism.* They bullied us, and otherwise discriminated. If they acknowledged we have been autistic, they'd look in a mirror. And, as discussed extensively throughout my memoir, up until this point, most people the mirror.

Hence, some students in my PhD cohort grew to hate me. Professors supported me, even though I didn't/don't respect authority. I knew a fuck ton of stuff, was intimidating, and spoke directly.

As you have already read for multiple chapters, you know my being seen as "the bad guy" during my PhD program was anything but a new thing for me. Them not liking me was not my first rodeo being seen as "the bad guy" for existing as myself and saying what I know. So honestly, it was fine. I couldn't have given any less fucks. At least when they socially discriminated against me for being autistic (and not realizing I was yet) I was now being seen as "the bad guy" for who I *actually fucking am.* It was progress, and I'd only begun then to be really proud of who I am.

Around this time, oddly enough, after at least 5 years of doing it, I finally decided to stop paying to get my hair bleached blonde and toned platinum, choosing to instead grow my roots Way back out to brunette. And I finally went to the dentist, for the first time in like, I don't know how long.

The first dentist tried to tell me I needed like seven fillings. I almost went with him and then at the last minute I got a really bad intuitive feeling, and I got a second opinion. The second said, I didn't need those fillings. This wasn't the first dentist who has trying to exploit me out of Goddess knows how much money to dig around in my mouth. So, I talked to someone about it and they recommended that I reported bad dentist to Big Teeth and, so, I did. Fuck bad dentist.

Around this time, I was drinking A LOT of whiskey most nights, after working myself most days from 8 am until 10:30 pm, just to manage all my responsibilities: coursework, teaching, and service work, that I struggled to uphold. I lived off of the downtown, and I would frequent going to this hole-in-the-wall bar on one side | venue on the other. I fucking loved that place. It was the one place I'd met people that I felt at home with, in the entire town. These were "my people" that I didn't think existed in this area of the Midwest. It was the closest thing to home I'd felt since leaving Chicagoland and moving there. So, I did what I often did, which is drink an incredible amount of whiskey, and then watch live music. I talked with many other locals who happened to sit at the bar. Some of them were grad. students. Others were just cismen who seemed to want to fuck me. And then there were just cool fucking regulars. One time I was there, and I was talking to an older "gentleman". He had a background in military and industry, and from talking to him, I learned that he was what's called a "Controller" at the University. And, his "Controller" job, for anyone that doesn't know what that means, is he decided how university money was used.

As soon as I learned this, I told a friend of mine at the time, because I was absolutely enthralled with learning, not only that this position exists at all, but also that they hired him because of what his background was in (that obviously informed how he's going to allocate that money). Controller told me he hated it, told me all about it, gave me his business card. I saw him times again after. Once, we talked about terrorism. Other times we just talked about whatever came up.

One night at this bar I showed up with my cool neighbor, and there was a comedy show happening on a tiny stage where sometimes shows were held. That night, there was a college boy comedian saying a bunch of really sexist ass shit, and so I started heckling him. He didn't like that. Eventually, the comedy show manager told me, "If you think you'd do better, come on up!"

And, so, I walked up to the microphone and I told all those fuckers exactly what I thought about them. And, while I was up at that mic, people started laughing at my commentary. Around this time, a few colleagues from the American Cultural Studies department walked in, and they started cheering for me. I can't thank them enough for that (if you're reading this, you know who you are). Anyway, after my ~ very first comedian set ever ~ I walked over to the people that were trying to boo me down during the set, and they said "you're actually really funny. That was real good". And I said "Thanks. But, you really gotta do something about sexist college kid". My neighbor had to of been so embarrassed, though. She couldn't possibly understand and it's OK.

If my having done this makes me "the bad guy" to some folks, I'm totally fine with it ¯_(ツ)_/¯

In March 2020, as we all know, COVID-19 hit the global fucking scene, and rocked all our lives differently, since. At the time, I was teaching a course in Writing for Electronic Media that I had never done before. So that semester halfway through an entirely new preparation course, I had to switch the course online and make it entirely asynchronous during a global fucking crisis, that I had no idea would not end. I had basically no money because I was getting paid $13,500 a year to teach two college classes as an instructor of record, and otherwise, living off of credit cards.

Poverty wasn't a new thing for me at all, at that point. I'd been poorer during my bachelors. I lived with basically no "essentials". And I didn't need "essentials," since I wasn't caring for myself. (I guess it was my own personal loophole. Real talk, though, I wouldn't recommend it.)

After I got the blood money from my mom's lung cancer lawsuit, and was living off of that full-time, I moved into a luxury apartment complex because my old apartment I'd lived in the first 2 years of my PhD had been making my nose bleed for like six months, and I never found out why.

All I knew was I need to get the fuck out of there. I had Twinkle again, and we deserved a Good Home **Goddess dammit**. After I moved in there, my life was mostly just a routine where I would exercise, cause I had a Peloton. I would make sure I ate really *really* well. All my water came in glass bottles or was filtered through a Berkey. I had all the things I could possibly desire and for the first time in – quite autist literally -- my entire life, while I was also taking care of myself.

Chapter Four.
Grieve Everything:
The Algorithmic
Envirusment

This chapter is dedicated to what I survived, and later realized, since the COVID-19 *envirusment* (environment + virus = *envirusment*) changed everything about my life, starting in March 2020.

The first entire year of COVID-19 was easily the most traumatizing "tower moment" of my life. I continued to attempt to be one of the first critical feminist media ecologists, inspired by the handful of other overshadowed or ostracized media ecologists doing similar work before our new wave of what, a handful of colleagues and I then, reductively, called "gender & media ecology". I grieved the life that I used to live, poor as absolute fuck, and did my best to adapt with still practically zero coping skills, no idea that I was emotionally projecting onto others, or money.

Due to a toxic ass cocktail of this, a week before I attended the 2020 virtual MEA convention and was invited to speak in the opening remarks of said convention, my advisor stepped down. Another mentor of mine stepped in as my chair, temporarily, which I was immensely grateful for. Then, my second committee member stepped down because of their own personal circumstances. And all this occurred during the summer I was working on an independent study with my third committee member, in preparation for the method section of my dissertation. I attended the convention as if nothing had happened because this was everything I ever loved, and the folks I had gotten to know the last few years within the Media Ecology Association are cool and great.

A couple days after the convention, I got a call from my mom. The following large segment was a first draft of a chapter that I wrote that was supposed to go into a timely edited collection on "Caregiving" that due to COVID, didn't end up panning out because :gestures at the year 2020:

Little did I know, that last week (as I was attending the 2020 virtual MEA convention) my mother had been having trouble sleeping laying down, went to the doctor to get looked at, and was being put on hospice. As far as we'd known, she was in remission, but now, she was stage-four cancer, and there was nothing more doctors could do for her besides end-of-life preparation.

I truly had no idea how to handle any of this. I lived three-and-a-half hour away from her and my dad, we all knew just how unreliable my fucking Sebring has become, and it was a global pandemic. She sounded "fine", besides some minor coughing. So, there was no way for me to process this experience at the time. One of the last things she said during that first phone call, announcing she would be put on hospice soon, was that she wanted to trade cars with me.

So, a week later, I made the drive with my title, and my mom and I exchanged cars. I wasn't sure if my falling apart Sebring would even make it there. But, thankfully it did, and despite some minor title issues, because of my distraught state, thanks to my mom, I was the owner of an SUV.

Due to the unknown status of the virus at the time, I didn't feel safe staying in the area because I didn't want to infect either of my parents. So, after exchanging vehicles, I drove back to Ohio. Not knowing what would happen with my mother's health, and not being able to do anything about it even if I wanted to, I escaped the panic by diving into my work. First thing was first, I strategized what I should do about my preliminary exam committee. According to my PhD handbook and the graduate college, I needed to complete my preliminary exams after completing my coursework. But now not knowing how much longer I would have left with my mom being on hospice (life expectancy 6 months) finishing coursework that Summer seemed far less likely.

After lots of thinking about what faculty members would work best for my project, I asked my remaining committee member to be my chair, and she accepted. Thankfully, she, as my new advisor, was exceptionally understanding of my circumstances. She supported me in taking an incomplete on the independent study with her that Summer, and helped me establish our other two committee members. I can honestly say, after all this difficulty, my committee couldn't possibly be in better shape for my exact project. Simultaneously, I proceeded to try and find out what my options were regarding coursework / preliminary exam deadline extensions and, eventually, to have a less strenuous graduate assistantship assignment for Fall 2020, to protect my mental and physical health and well-being, all traumatic things happening to me considered.

A few weeks of frantic reading and annotating later, my dad called. My mom had suddenly, and drastically worsened, and was now unable to muster energy to even use her phone by herself.

As shown in the above post, a loved one dying of
cancer within a dysfunctional family, doesn't
magically alleviate any prior familial
dysfunctions, even during the context of
unprecedentedly tragic times. The following two
images are of a poem I wrote called "EVERY

NIGHT," about driving to visit with my mom.

EVERY NIGHT

My father
Sleeps a
Few feet
Away from
Where my
Mom died.

Weeks before
Her official
Passing he had
Pronounced her
Already dead.

Stopped
Listening to
Her voice,

Properly
Feeding her,

Or treating
Her like
Human.

———

I arrived to
Find her in
A Shrunken
State. jaw
and collar
Bones

Subdued
Into near
Silence.

Luckily,

I'm not
Deterred
So easily
By quiet.

———

For days,
I asked
Her ?s &
Listened
To her
Shallow
Breathe
Struggles
To string 2-
3 words, &
Make more
Sense than
My father
Would give
Her credit.

———

I heard her,
And the more
I heard her, the
More she spoke,
The more she ate,
The more energy she
Exuded, Until she was
Fashioning the wit & person
I had always known, but never
Took the time to appreciate in
A fullness death introduces you
To of those you never loved loud
Enough, soon enough, lively enough.

———

To be honest, I have no memory of time that lapsed after sending some emails July 29th, 2020, until August 10th, 2020, when my dad called. I tried to finish coursework. The following images tweets, and the last section of EVERY NIGHT, detailing my experiences from that time.

Bernadette "bird" Bowen, ABD
@BBowenBGSU

Replying to @BBowenBGSU

Because of this news, I was stuck between an impossibly dehumanizing place of either: a) driving 4 hours back to Ohio without going to my parents house OR b) risking exposure to my own COVID (or exposing them, since IDK if I'm positive either) to be there when my mom would die.

10:00 AM · Aug 11, 2020 · Twitter for iPhone

Bernadette "bird" Bowen, ABD
@BBowenBGSU

Yesterday my dad called me and suggested I drive home because my mom's body was shutting down.

I drove 4 hours there only to learn that one of her home health aids was exposed to COVID and had since spent all night with her.

9:49 AM · Aug 11, 2020 · Twitter for iPhone

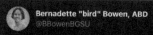
Bernadette "bird" Bowen, ABD
@BBowenBGSU

Replying to @BBowenBGSU

I decided to say my goodbyes before I drove back.

My mother could barely be considered conscious when I saw her last.

I don't know if she could hear me, but I held her still warm hand and stroked her hair as she laid there.

I washed my hands frantically before and after.

10:03 AM · Aug 11, 2020 · Twitter for iPhone

Bernadette "bird" Bowen, ABD
@BBowenBGSU

Replying to @BBowenBGSU

I had already planned to sleep in my car, but now the one place in the state that was safe for me to use a restroom had likely been exposed to this virus.

To be clear, I don't blame the health aid, I blame the U.S government which has refused to responsibly shutdown the country.

9:56 AM · Aug 11, 2020 · Twitter for iPhone

Bernadette "bird" Bowen, ABD
@BBowenBGSU

Replying to @BBowenBGSU

The one aspect of peace I had is that I saw her and reminded her how much I love her a few weeks ago, before she'd reached this state. It mostly felt futile repeating myself in her current state. I know she already knew what I'd say. What was important is that I was there at all.

10:07 AM · Aug 11, 2020 · Twitter for iPhone

Bernadette "bird" Bowen, ABD
@BBowenBGSU

Replying to @BBowenBGSU

Afterward I talked with my dad and the hospice nurses a bit about the absurdity of this situation, I drove back to Ohio.

The drive was mostly crying and disassociation, but I made it back to the area, and I planned to pick up something for dinner after the exhausting day.

10:10 AM · Aug 11, 2020 · Twitter for iPhone

Bernadette "bird" Bowen, ABD
@BBowenBGSU

Replying to @BBowenBGSU

Shortly after I pulled into the parking lot, I got a call from my dad that my mom had died.

My dad is a Vietnam War veteran, who I've seen cry maybe 3 times in my life (at his own parents funerals, and yesterday apologizing that I'd driven all that way to his unsafe home.)

10:13 AM · Aug 11, 2020 · Twitter for iPhone

Bernadette "bird" Bowen, ABD
@BBowenBGSU

Replying to @BBowenBGSU

The point of my disclosing all of this isn't for pity or to receive prayers or whatever else. To be honest, those sentiments don't do anything for me.

Fixing this broken fucking system would do something for me and everyone else who's experiencing death of loved ones right now.

10:15 AM · Aug 11, 2020 · Twitter for iPhone

Bernadette "bird" Bowen, ABD
@BBowenBGSU

Replying to @BBowenBGSU

This pandemic was bad enough already.

There is no fucking excuse anyone can tell me right now, or ever again, that justifies the American government's decision to not shutdown the economy and pay us financial relief so more of us don't die.

What the fuck is it going to take?

10:18 AM · Aug 11, 2020 · Twitter for iPhone

Bernadette "bird" Bowen, ABD
@BBowenBGSU

Replying to @BBowenBGSU

That home health aid SHOULD NoT have had to go to work and contract the fucking virus, and then Inevitably carry it to people's sick and dying loved ones. If this pandemic was handled by America anywhere between March-July I could have been there when my mom died.

But it wasn't.

10:20 AM · Aug 11, 2020 · Twitter for iPhone

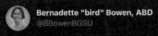

Bernadette "bird" Bowen, ABD
@BBowenBGSU

Replying to @BBowenBGSU

Today my sister and dad are consulting about what kind of funeral arrangements for my mom can be feasibly and safely executed during a global pandemic.

No one should be having to do this.

The blood of these grotesquely inhumane circumstances is on the U.S governments hands.

10:30 AM · Aug 11, 2020 · Twitter for iPhone

I heard her
Until I couldn't.
And then I drove
The four hours there
To hold her hand, as she
Laid dying, and I couldn't
Feel her there any longer,
And felt little need to speak
Any truths she hadn't already
Heard. I drove four hours back,
And as soon as I arrived safely,
In the SUV she gifted me to keep,
My father called, and she was gone.

The following weeks, much like the former ones, were a blur of supportive phone calls, sobbing, social media posting, disassociation, random gift and meal drop offs by my nearby loved ones, and my complete and total inability to function on a basic level. Despite our tenuous relationship, losing my mom during the start of COVID floored me unlike anything ever has. Adding grotesque corporatism to this tragedy, a week before she passed, she told my sister and I that she had signed a non-disclosure agreement about suing companies responsible for her lung cancer.

At the time she revealed this, I wasn't sure when I would receive my allotment of this blood money that my mom worked so hard to ensure her daughters received in place of her life. But, in the meantime, I responded to learning about this corporate settlement for poisoning my mom to death like the critical scholar whose conducted research on corporate corruption that I am: by connecting the dots I've learned about corporatized education and general U.S. injustices.

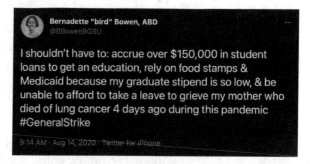

Bernadette "bird" Bowen, ABD
@BBowenBGSU

I shouldn't have to: accrue over $150,000 in student loans to get an education, rely on food stamps & Medicaid because my graduate stipend is so low, & be unable to afford to take a leave to grieve my mother who died of lung cancer 4 days ago during this pandemic #GeneralStrike

9:14 AM · Aug 14, 2020 · Twitter for iPhone

A few days later, we learned that a hospice aid who stayed with my mom the whole night before she passed away had tested positive for COVID-19. And then my dad tested positive as well.

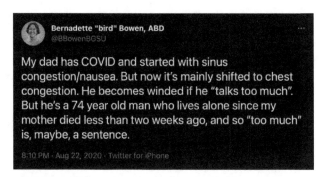

At the same time, all my required graduate college deadlines were beginning to wear on me, detrimentally. To make matters more complicated, a few weeks into Fall 2020 after all the work I put forth to not teach so I could grieve my mom's death, I was asked by my department head to pick up a 4000-level dream course from my chair, who was approved to take a CARES leave.

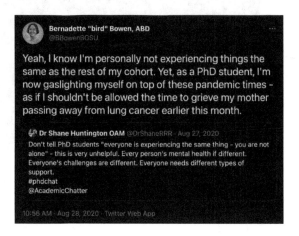

Meanwhile, my entire family didn't know if my dad would also die of COVID-19 only one week of my mother having passed away. And, so, for sake of the overall health and well-being of those who planned to attend my mom's wake, we were faced with little to no choice, but to post-pone her wake / funeral until a month after her death. Thankfully, by then, my dad had recovered well.

But it was an ongoing global pandemic and, thus, wasn't safe for me to stay in the area after.

And, just as my mom's hospice process didn't lack family dysfunction, neither did her wake.

Bernadette "bird" Bowen, ABD
@BBowenBGSU

Shout out to my sister who cry yelled and kicked out our racist trump supporting uncle because he refused to wear a mask at my mom's wake.

9:40 AM · Oct 4, 2020 · Twitter for iPhone

Once my mom's wake was over, and I drove back to Ohio, the next deadline on my stressful ass to do list was preparing for and scheduling preliminary exams with my newly minted committee, alongside a host of other responsibilities I needed to accomplish to become a job candidate.

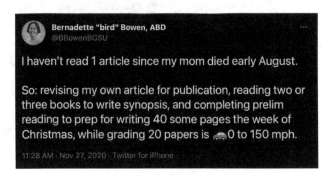

Bernadette "bird" Bowen, ABD
@BBowenBGSU

I haven't read 1 article since my mom died early August.

So: revising my own article for publication, reading two or three books to write synopsis, and completing prelim reading to prep for writing 40 some pages the week of Christmas, while grading 20 papers is 0 to 150 mph.

11:28 AM · Nov 27, 2020 · Twitter for iPhone

As you can imagine, this tragic and stressful series of events has hit home unlike any reading ever had regarding cruelties of the corporatized education structure. And my observations prior to this were already rather grim. I did what I had to do to jump through bureaucratic hoops and attempt to solidify my future. But I wasn't interested in pretending as if what I have experienced was anywhere near "okay". Holistically, and as wise feminists have reported occurs for centuries, the loss of my mother affected me both personally and politically as my life proceeded on.

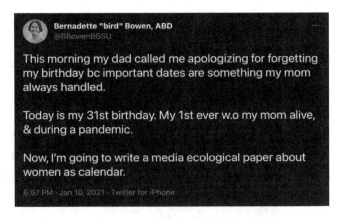

Bernadette "bird" Bowen, ABD
@BBowenBGSU

This morning my dad called me apologizing for forgetting my birthday bc important dates are something my mom always handled.

Today is my 31st birthday. My 1st ever w.o my mom alive, & during a pandemic.

Now, I'm going to write a media ecological paper about women as calendar.

6:57 PM · Jan 10, 2021 · Twitter for iPhone

My experiences continue to inform the ways I view the U.S. response to this pandemic. For example, the ways in which I've seen higher education prioritize profit over people thus far.

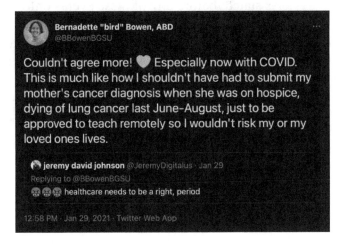

Bernadette "bird" Bowen, ABD
@BBowenBGSU

Couldn't agree more! 🖤 Especially now with COVID. This is much like how I shouldn't have had to submit my mother's cancer diagnosis when she was on hospice, dying of lung cancer last June-August, just to be approved to teach remotely so I wouldn't risk my or my loved ones lives.

jeremy david johnson @JeremyDigitalus · Jan 29
Replying to @BBowenBGSU
😤😤😤 healthcare needs to be a right, period

12:58 PM · Jan 29, 2021 · Twitter Web App

As time went on, I learned that my remote accommodations, that I was granted were deemed "illegitimate" past May. And, that if I wanted accommodations I needed to reapply. Between a history of "severe allergies", I thought made me ineligible to receive the C19 mRNA vaccines, I consulted my doctor and reapplied for official accommodations, but was, repeatedly, denied.

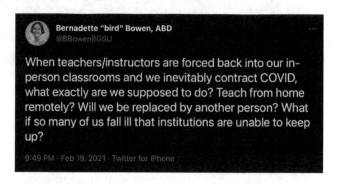

When teachers/instructors are forced back into our in-person classrooms and we inevitably contract COVID, what exactly are we supposed to do? Teach from home remotely? Will we be replaced by another person? What if so many of us fall ill that institutions are unable to keep up?

9:49 PM · Feb 19, 2021 · Twitter for iPhone

As stated, before any of these events unfolded, I had been reading, studying, and writing about the consequences of neoliberal late-stage capitalism. But until the COVID-19 *envirusment* rocked my world, I truly never anticipated the ways in which the costs of this system would hit home. As many universities, and other essential workplaces, have shown, human lives are less important than an increase in their bottom line. The loss of over one million U.S. lives has since been rationally dismissed as if they were all expendable casualties to the dehumanizing economy.

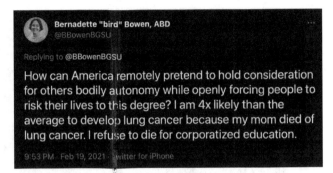

Although my sister and I received monetary
compensation (aforementioned blood money)
from the corporations that poisoned my mother to
death (because of her hard work and efforts to
grasp a single sense of ownership regarding her
lung cancer and impending death), I now
additionally offer a uniquely perverse insider
perspective on U.S. legal systems enabling for-
profit murder.

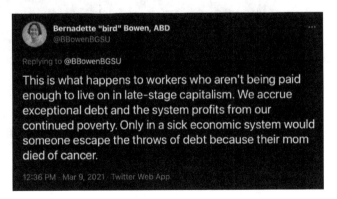

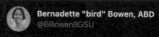
Bernadette "bird" Bowen, ABD
@BBowenBGSU

···

At the end of every semester since starting graduate school I've had to take out a few thousand dollars in loans from this company called Elastic to just survive on the bare minimum. Now that I'm not using it anymore they're constantly emailing me like,"...wait, aren't you poor?"

12:33 PM · Mar 9, 2021 · Twitter Web App

Bernadette "bird" Bowen, ABD
@BBowenBGSU

···

Replying to @BBowenBGSU

My mom is one of hundreds of other lung cancer patients who had the where-with-all to contact a lawyer and sue companies that willingly poison citizens for profit. It's demented to me that I will now not be homeless in my fourth year of my PhD because my mom sued before she died.

12:39 PM · Mar 9, 2021 · Twitter Web App

Bernadette "bird" Bowen, ABD
@BBowenBGSU

···

Replying to @BBowenBGSU

Recently, I contacted the law firm handling my mom's settlements to inquire a list of companies knowingly responsible for countless deaths from this for-profit poisoning. The paralegal informed me that many of the companies end up closing and never even being held accountable.

12:43 PM · Mar 9, 2021 · Twitter Web App

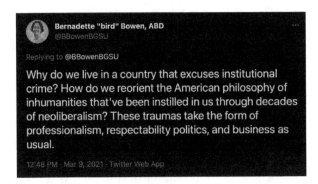

Bernadette "bird" Bowen, ABD
@BBowenBGSU

Replying to @BBowenBGSU

Why do we live in a country that excuses institutional crime? How do we reorient the American philosophy of inhumanities that've been instilled in us through decades of neoliberalism? These traumas take the form of professionalism, respectability politics, and business as usual.

12:48 PM · Mar 9, 2021 · Twitter Web App

Prior to writing this (supposed to be book) chapter, I approached these compounding traumas creatively, by publishing a micro-chapbook about before, during, and after the loss of my mother.

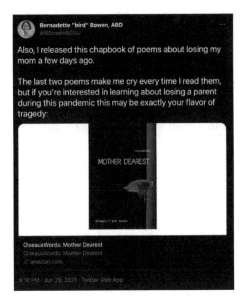

Bernadette "bird" Bowen, ABD
@BBowenBGSU

Also, I released this chapbook of poems about losing my mom a few days ago.

The last two poems make me cry every time I read them, but if you're interested in learning about losing a parent during this pandemic this may be exactly your flavor of tragedy:

MOTHER DEAREST

OiseauxWords: Mother Dearest
OiseauxWords: Mother Dearest
& amazon.com

4:10 PM · Jun 29, 2021 · Twitter Web App

(To learn the fullest picture of that grieving process, read my above poetry micro-chapbook.)

Grieving An Unjust World? Let's TikTalk About It

About a year into COVID-19, I started seeing A LOT of TikTok tarot readers. I always wanted to know how to read tarot myself. As a proud gypsy, it always intrigued me. So, I taught myself tarot, and I have read my own tarot cards ever since. It has been one of the single most effective methods in my building any sense of my own spiritual practice, reflecting on who I've been, what I didn't deserve, alongside reminders that I always deserved to be treated better, and to develop boundaries, to release the weight and/or mistreated of all the people existing around me. (Besides the time I was accused of burning down the barn with witchcraft, this practice has been the single most positively influential experience of my own version of spirituality I've ever had.)

2021 was also when I wrote my dissertation in five months. But what I, actually, mean when I say that is that after four years of my research, across a span five months I didn't work for the first 3 weeks then I'd write a chapter at the end of each month. During my PhD, I realized I could feasibly write an entire paper in about four days - - if I really needed to. In that way, my PhD program, although grueling, taught me what I was capable of because of my autistic hyper focus, pattern recognition, and comprehensive dedication to my research. At that time, I knew I was autistic, and began reprocessing how much of a living hell that my autism had made my life a lot of the time, but also provided me impressive and useful capabilities to write what I need to write.

Maybe it was my teen years of blogging from my very millennial upbringing. Maybe it was all the tricks I used to get myself to write after I stared at a blank page too long, adapting to the "blank canvas effect". At that point in my life, I had written in fucking Facebook notes, when those still existed. (Right now, I'm talk to texting into the notes section of my iPhone because that's the easiest way I can get myself to "do the writing". I've had to learn to adapt to write past basically any barriers my body had set. So, now, I get to reap the benefits -- God damn it! 😁)

The world was now in my exceptionally over-washed hands from taking COVID-19 precautions.

My hands

Said to me,

"You have
Forgotten
You are an
Ecosystem.

…Let me…
…..Remind
———You."

—-

When
Disinfecting
With alcohol

You
deaden
All living

Things
Inside
Alive.

—-

Water
Your
Ponds

& in
Habit

Your
Body,

Little
Planet.

—-

Circulate
Around
Your own
————sun.

That One Time I Remembered and Forgave Myself For Being Many "Me"s

In the *envirusment*, I realized in my teens and twenties I'd come home and immediately go to my room. I needed nothing more than to be left alone after being perpetually overstimulated by life. I also always had a hard time taking care of myself because of my PDA autism and related trauma.

Now, it's 2023, and I don't remember the feeling of another person's nearby presence, let alone touch. Not besides behind a screen. The risk of a haircut in a nation that re-embraced eugenics.

Outside parts of the world, that I'd frequented prior to 2020, haven't been safe for over 3 years.

And it's well documented we'd long been in epidemics of touch hunger, loneliness, and less sex.

The most social interaction I had during 2020-2022 was being on the all-audio app Clubhouse.

I have been almost completely and utterly alone to reprocess and reflect on my life for 3 years.

In doing so, I see the *envirusment* revealed foundationally "normal" mediated dehumanizations.

Turns out reembracing eugenics has been easy to do for most folks I thought I knew in the U.S.

Just as easy as sexual violence are to normalize and never criminalize. Bodily autonomy, who?

In a sick, undeniable, sense, these last 3 years could be seen as my redo. A barrier between what I'd done and what I will never do again. (I always had sex with cismen. Most likely, not again.)

As an unrealized neuroqueer person, I lived and "loved" the first 30 years of my life taught to be and live near completely boundaryless. All chapters until this point have been my own retelling regarding how my life was before I realized who I am. And it shouldn't have ever been this way.

Recently I've come to the realization that I don't blame my family for not knowing what autism is before psychologists even did. They didn't stand a chance in knowing, despite all my lifelong signs. They couldn't know how undiagnosed and diversely experienced autism has always been.

Likewise, I forgive almost every person in this book I've included, except, of course, my rapists. Know that this process of reprocessing and revisiting my life has been a therapeutic healthy act.

A Dr. bird's Eye View on Self-Realizations in the Algorithmic *Envirusment*

One of the major findings of my dissertation about sociosexual ecologies in the algorithmic age is that there have been massive neuroqueer self-realizations happening on algorithmic platforms.

In multiple publications since finishing my PhD, I have discussed various implications of this.

(See my Academia.edu page for free copies of all of my publications, and sources stated herein.)

We are only beginning to understand the gravity of recent findings about lost autist generations.

What I've done throughout this memoir is autopsy my own lifetime of flesh to demonstrate that.

Namely, it was easy for me to not to know who I am, when an estimate of up to 80% of "me"s have also been missed. And it wasn't for my lack of trying or lack of needs. Many of us can't afford to get a diagnosis, literally or socially, because of how ableist the world has always been and remains today. Did you know 9 out of 10 AFAB autists experience sexual violence anyway?

It speaks volumes looking back at my early life and remembering the casual discrimination I was raised into from birth. I've always hyper-fixated on it. I needed to know everything about how humans, language, and society worked, so that I could survive. The ways that, without knowing I was autistic (and, even if I did) I couldn't possibly have known the ecological interconnections of the society that existed -- long before I got here. In hindsight, what made my lifelong process of observing, and attempting to mask, that much more complicated was that I have alexithymia, hyper-empathy, and interoception issues. So, not only could I not identify my own emotions, but I have difficulty determining any feelings in body until they reach about a nine on a feeling scale.

But I also didn't know any of these terms, or that this happened, so just I blushed – hard – for, basically, my entire fucking life. Because turns out, when you're having feelings, even if you can't identify or pinpoint that you're feeling them, they still express themselves, somehow. And for me, that looked like blushing all over my face and even down my stomach. And, sometimes, fortunately, but other times, rather unfortunately, people have interpreted my visibly expressed feelings to mean something I was in fact not feeling. And then, unfortunately, I didn't know too.

Historically, this society wasn't made to see AFAB folks as any more than, at absolute best, an accessory to a full human being, who then is socialized to go on and become pregnant and carry babies. It didn't matter what I really "felt". Paired with my autism, folks were more than happy to tell me what I was feeling for me. And if/when I didn't correct them, my silence spoke for me.

(And plus, as they are experienced, feelings of any kind are much more ambiguous than folks often realize. And that's because most don't consider the insufficient nature of language, due to the "God Trick" farce passed off by science specializations, designed to quantify abstract ideas.

In other words, the categories we use to describe things have never been the things themselves.)

Embodied sexuality can also be triggering for autists who have been taught they're not allowed to move their body in the ways they're naturally inclined to move. If we are so deeply masked after a lifetime of internalized ableism (not even knowing we're autistic — to boot--) we're more likely to then not allow ourselves to move in moments that are supposed to be intimate, where we're intended to embrace our embodied presence and experience free movement and pleasure.

However, sex with cismen, when I mistook myself for a ciswoman, was mostly unorgasmic at best, and violence, at worst. In hindsight, I did anything I could to avoid doing it in relationships. To this day, I'm not sure I ever wanted to have sex with them because it became so unbearably unworthy of my fucking time to go through the motions, time and time again, and not actually receive a reciprocally enjoyable experience. Most of the time, at any age, sex with cismen was me laboring a pornographic mask for a few minutes. Feeding their ego was easy. Treating them like their body wasn't something to be ashamed of, because, of course, only mine was. Assuring them I would internalize, all their ugly parts for them. As far as I could tell, they truly never even considered doing the same for me. Do you wanna know why I know that they didn't? Because they never did for 30 years. I have r** poem, after r** poem, after r** poem to show for it. My piece "Requirement Politics", my dissertation, and a failed start at a case for false imprisonment.

Yet zero Justice. My one Dr. bird's eye view, alone, could never represent everyone. But now, knowing 9 out of 10 AFAB autists experienced sexual violence, I see folks lived similar pains.

All these issues in tandem are also the reason I never felt like I could say anything about it. It's hard enough for any white non-disabled AFAB to receive legal justice for their cases of sexual violence when they fit a textbook description of some "masked monster". I know, as any sexual violence researcher does, the vast majority of perpetrators never spend a day in jail. (Not that the current carceral system could ever provide the best answer. But any amount of criminalization (and ideally, rehabilitation) would be better than the practically none that has been the norm.)

Knowing what I know now about the creations of whiteness, disability, gender, etc. has given me a very unique and empowering perspective of this world. We've also long been influenced by a media industry, that exploits young folk's bodies, dressing, and presenting kids as overtly sexualized adults. By the time puberty rolled around for me, I had a computer in my room, and also was taught my body was disgusting and to be altered to meet cisheteronormative standards (legs/armpits/everything shaved, makeup applied, eyebrows waxed, bodies covered, no farting, shitting, periods hidden, as if they all aren't natural experiences) or else I'd face social rejection.

Yet, cisheteronormative pressures alone were – nothing -- compared to body micromanagement I'd undergone as an unrealized neuroqueer enby. Autism both makes me who I am *and* my life a living hell. It's been 3 years since my mom died of lung cancer. I'm 33 as I write this now, and only began to learn who I am at 30. I didn't know who I was until she died. I didn't know who I was until the world fell apart and algorithms worked their crisis mode datafied magic. I fell for the binaries too. Lucky for us all, gender identity is fluid and people can change their identities throughout their lives, if they allow themselves to embrace different versions of themselves.

Why? It's well documented that, especially non-disabled Black and Brown, queer, AFAB folks are delegitimized, overshadowed, ignored, or erased in every facet of the current structure from education and legislation to medicine. Now, we see the algorithmic *envirusment* has blown the U.S. foundation open, and most everyone alive is totally ignoring post-COVID ailments, and long-COVID, as well as disabled people dying of it, unless they become disabled themselves. Now, we know autists are both more common and high risk for COVID-19 (due to the incredibly long list of comorbidities that we often also have along autism) than once thought. Do the math!

To be clear, each type of "neurodivergence" (a term I do not like because it mostly reinforces a reductive neurotype binary) faces criticisms and stigmas. And as disability activists and scholars repeat, especially schizophrenia and bipolar. In order to begin unpacking this pathologization, autistic academics in particular have been making large strides to destigmatize what autism is.

However, the difficulty of doing that is no small task. And, as a media and communication PhD, I know this is because the English language itself is a media so biased, with ableisms so deeply built in, that roads (which seem to lead away from ableisms) in fact, lead directly back into them.

For instance, the autists who have gotten the most traction, support, and notoriety on algorithmic platforms, thus far, are predominantly white folks, who are verbal, and conventionally attractive. And, as a critical media ecologist, I know that is because the algorithms have the same fucking biases built into them as all other physical, virtual, and algorithmic mediations. This is also why colonial capitalist "palatable" autism has become the focus of a common understanding of "neurodivergent" when in fact, even that insufficient word means much more than just "autism".

As in you cannot use "autism" and "neurodivergent" synonymously. (Well, you can, but that's inaccurate.) Instead, "neurodiversity" is an orientational shift into understanding and acting from a knowing that the binary of neurodivergent and neurotypical was always insufficient. Meaning, what we (all folks deemed "neurodivergent" or "neurotypical") really need is a "neurodiversity" that embraces the inherent worth of, not only all autists, but all neurotypes and all body-minds.

(It was brought to my attention recently this term was wrongly accredited to TERF Judy Singer, when in fact it was a term developed on an autistic forum before Singer, that was called InLv.)

Because that has yet to be done, beyond neoliberal institutions cherry-picking and doing the bare minimum to make "neurodiversity" a buzzword (as all corporatized institutions are known to do), instead we're in the context in which eugenics has returned, opening the door to fascism.

It's been eye opening to learn that Nazi eugenicists were who decided that any autists profitable to capitalism wouldn't be systematically eliminated. But this time around, fascists are affording us all "equal opportunity" lack of basics, autonomy, climate crisis, and death from COVID-19.

If we were honest, I think most of us would admit that we have been socialized into being *the bad guy* in this terribly inequitable world. This doesn't excuse discriminatory ideas and behavior that must, eventually and meticulously, be unlearned for us to build and live in a liberated world.

This is why through critical media ecology, I repeat my three tenants: We only know we know, Everything becomes normal repetition, and Everything is connected. What I've learned from my Dr. bird's eye view is nothing new. It's similar to what Indigenous folks and other historically and intentionally targeted marginalized groups have said forever, that: these colonially-founded capitalist-funded neoliberal corporatized systems have disconnected us to most of our detriments.

You might be thinking, why does that matter? It matters, even if you are not formally educated because any way of thinking or being from "traditional" perspectives and scopes (that inform our entire environment) incline a disregard for the overall ecological interconnectedness of all things.

Need I remind you, the UN report that came out on April 1st, 2023, warned we now have 10 years to make enormous structural changes to colonial capitalism, if we want to survive as a species, avoiding the climate warming point of no return. I am sharing what I've learned because despite the ongoing terror of increasing U.S. fascism, we still have time to do that. I can't believe I have to say this, but only a fascist media bastardizes the idea that being "anti-fascist" is wrong.

To think that, so seamlessly, the current transnational and global media landscape was able to contaminate the public's imaginary, reversing such basic things is terrifyingly "New Normal".

Blood-relatedly, for the last decade, I haven't been able to know my many nieces and nephews because of multiple instances in which my sister and her husband have made it clear I'm not welcome around her children, since I believe people assigned female at birth belong in role of leadership, like cismen. About a month ago, we had a conversation where she expressed that we should just "agree to disagree". She actually had the nerve to say we only didn't get along just because our dead mom "made both of us sound worse as a mediator than we ever were". So, then I asked her a question. I asked, "So, do you or do you not believe that people assigned female at birth belong in roles of leadership like cismen?" She proceeded to ask me what "cismen" means. I answered her in a very straightforward way, as I am known for doing. She said she "doesn't believe in that". I told her I'm non-binary, a woman, gender, sexuality specialist, and that her opinion doesn't change the fact that it and I exist as non-binary. Her source for that was an article from a right wing think tank that claimed, "only two sexes" and "biological women" exist.

Again, by the time we had this conversation, I hadn't had a real conversation with her in almost 10 years. And it made me I remember why. After she invalidated my gender, I told her "I refuse to have anyone in my life that disrespects any element of my identity". And she messaged back: "So, what, if Dad dies, you don't want me to tell you?" So, I asked her back "Don't you see how manipulative that was?" Then she gaslit me as if I made a big deal out of nothing, I put my "Do not disturb" on, and she continued to send multiple texts, then admitting that she doesn't believe anyone assigned female at birth belongs in the roles of leadership like cismen because "Bible".

For all these connected reasons (and more!),
readers, my early life had Bern'd me the fuck out.

Part Three.
Dr. bird

Chapter Five. Neuroqueer Mass Self-Realizations: Now What?

What if I told you that as a sociologically trained media & communication PhD, that in certain respects, I'm more credible to talk about the COVID-19 *envirusment* than anyone at the CDC, virologists, and epidemiologists AND also more credible about autism than most psychologists?

This is bold. But hold your skepticism for just a minute to hear me out…The *envirusment* results from sickening, disabling, and deadly social and communication norms. U.S. institutions that are responsible for protecting us, prioritized profit over all our lives, failing as in every imaginable way, generating a landscape of anti-mask and overly utopian vaccine [long-] COVID-19 denial.

To contextualize this, allow me to remind everyone about the fact that (despite the abysmal state of things) this is the very first time in history we have been this interconnected (the COVID-19 *envirusment* has revealed that *as* a media), literally and figuratively, and have the capabilities, thanks to technological advancements to make quick systemic changes, if and when we choose.

So, again, we know autism is massively undiagnosed, and countless people have been missed. We know many late-in-life realized autists can't afford, or would be harmed more than benefit from, receiving a formal diagnosis because of the ongoing eugenics context. We, also, know that upwards of 80% of AFAB autists are undiagnosed by the age of 18. We, *also also*, know that 75-85% of autists are unemployed due to systemic discrimination against us (since we know that that 75% goes to 85% after we earn a college degree). We, *also also also*, know that non-autistic people, systemically and socially, discriminate against autistic people. We, *also also also also*, know many autists have higher rates of substance abuse and suicidality. We, *also also also also also*, know at least 9 out of 10 AFAB autists live sexually violent lives. We, *also also also also also also*, know that autists have an increasingly long list of highly likely comorbidities that put us at significantly higher risk for general health complications, and a severe case of COVID-19. And we know autists are often, neuroqueer, whether that be gender and/or [no] attraction type. Therefore, we've never been better informed/equipped to end systemic discrimination of autists.

However, these findings have primarily been treated as if they're not in fact all connected. So, in this memoir, I dissected my own substance abusing, sexually violated life as one late-in-life realized autist, demonstrating how my own experiences exemplify a sexually violent U.S. body politic. Unfortunately for all of us, thanks to colonial-founded / capitalist-funded dehumanizations built into the system as features: we only knew what we knew, everything became normal in repetition, and all of it (and more!) was connected. And, so, mass neuroqueer self-realizations occurring in the algorithmic *envirusment* do, in fact, have vast individual/systemic implications.

Secondly, as a collective, we have never held this much tangible power to actually fix the deeply inequitable structures that this nation and globe were built upon. Although, the most of us have been disinformed and miseducated about topics from sex ed to race, we still have never had such a ripe opportunity to fix everything that's happening, that continues to literally kill us — daily.

Thirdly, we owe it to ourselves and others to remember that academic specialties and topics of study, everything from medicine to education (and — truly — just about every institution that currently exists) have been built deliberately inequitably. Thus, we need to have accountability for these issues because without that, we cannot, and — truly — should not, move forward.

Said in another way, we can't understand the exact COVID-19 *envirusment* moment that we are dealing with, right now, each and every day, without first reckoning with the very *human mediated* and equally taken for granted commutative reasons why there is anti-intellectualism.

In short, what I argue in my work, it is that we are in a remarkable time in which the previous forms of authority are colliding with online influencers, and other user-based following-fueled forms of expertise. Lucky for us, I argue in my work that this aspect is for better and for worse.

Much like COVID-19 has revealed to us our interconnectedness through the ongoing trauma and ailments spread through our airways, this understandably historical skepticism of traditional authorities is eye-opening. This era illuminates ways we can and must close the authority gap.

And, as readers saw in my cut-the-shit memoir, I say this as a millennial, born and raised into all of these deeply discriminatory norms (ableism, racism, cisheterosexism, etc.) who continues to work to painstakingly unlearn all these

dehumanizations that our inequitable society sells
to us.

This is all to say, that until we expand beyond the
aforementioned narrow, non-Objective, and/or
un-universalizable criteria of who has ever been
allowed to be an authority — who experts have
always been and who they can be — we will not
move forward without more needless sickness,
disablement and death for profit. We will also fail
countless people, just like the autism criteria.

Academic literature has always lagged behind the
most recent research findings by at least a few
years. It has never been clearer, that we cannot
afford to wait any longer to solve these problems.

The Story

This is the
story of
how we
keep living.

—-

These, our
stories. Us,
Cursing 🐑
Mortalities.

—-

This is a
story of

dying as
The only
—kept—
promise.

With now well over 1 million U.S. citizens alone
needlessly dead and continuing to die from
COVID-19 (and countless more disabled by long-
COVID, being ignored) to protect the economy
exploiting us all to the fullest extent of the law,
the government - made of disinformed and
miseducated people — has done nothing but
shown us that it cares nothing for our health /
lives.

Lastly, the cherry on this hellscape, need I remind
everyone, we are also hurdling towards the
climate apocalypse. None of this is hyperbole.
Fuck, I wish it was! All scientifically legitimate
signs show COVID-19 and the climate
apocalypse are our ongoing realities. The
sickening, disabling, and deadly media and
communicative denial of both of these crises are
issues created and sustained by colonial capitalist
logics and practices that always dehumanized the
bulk of us.

What more does the U.S. public need to see to understand that this system is not working for the most of us? We have infinitely more to gain from ensuring the planet remains habitable to all of us than the few thousand billionaires who profit, the most from the current system, have to lose. The current colonially-founded, neoliberal capitalist economy must mean nothing in comparison to the massive loss of all our lives and the destruction of our ability to live on this planet. We cannot move our entire species to Mars, colonizing there too. How many more must become disabled and die before we demand to change everything colonially-founded / capitalist-funded?

I have nothing but the utmost respect for any psychologists, virologists, epidemiologists, and climate scientists who have made it their life's works to conduct rigorous liberatory-based research and have told only the sickening, disabling, and deadly truths over the last 3 years about COVID-19, autism, and the climate, *AND* they're all a result of deadly human mediated norms.

That's what makes the *envirusment* novel. Thanks to the Internet (and the many *many* people whose lives works have come before me), we are able to connect, and can turn this car around.

And, most urgently, get out of the metaphorical car onto the color-paved racist infrastructure built by enslaved people, colonizers called the United States, and give land back to Indigenous folks who so clearly have always known how to take care of it much better than colonizers do.

Besides my three critical media ecological tenants, that main take away I have learned from all my life personally and politically is that: people who look back for his-story to repeat itself are always facing the wrong way, and they forget to see what media(s) exist right in front of them.

Admittedly, I am biased in that I have, for most of my life, held a lifelong disrespect for history. It was only until graduate school that I learned about critical strands of the field, and its cousin's philosophy of science, philosophy of technology, philosophy of medicine, etc. that I saw the necessities in viewing the past(s) to understanding musings of the present and possible futures.

Now What? From My Dr. bird's Eye View

As a media and communication scholar (and specifically as one of the first ever critical media ecologists), one of my main concerns now is that I see people constrain their own views, looking backward, and it leads them to forget we exist an entirely different media era. As especially critical cultural scholars of media and media ecologists have explicated, this assemblage of digital and algorithmic spaces has dramatically altered ways we can/do relate to surroundings.

This is why, one of my biggest ongoing COVID-19 era *envirusment* pet peeves is that if/when I persistently see and hear people talking about ideas, processes, institutions, and/or events of the past as if they would constrain and replicate what could be done in our future. It's just not true.

And, this is why, for two main reasons, I beg everyone who looks to the past for future insights to stop doing this. First, because we have to remember that our foundations were equivocally corrupted by humans *as* media (specifically, the Enlightenment model). Thus, what has been done must not be referred to as a "natural", "Objective", or "universal" default for what is possible. Meaning, if we look to the past as what can be done now or later, we forget the potentialities for any one of the linguistic blueprints they wrought have always been little more than mythical constructs of "grandeur". For example, the idea that we have identified the "greatest minds" of history is as much of a fiction as the idea that "time equals money". This language usage as media, like a blueprint of ways we *see* and *do*, ideologically cover that in inequitable systems, one white cisman's beauty has always been another person's breakdown.

(I talk about this much more extensively in my "Requirement Politics" article mentioned earlier.)

Secondly, the ever-increasingly speed at which advancements have been and continue to be made, have also dramatically changed how quickly any and all mediated changes (social, political, financial, structural) can now be made. In other words, especially now in the ongoing COVID-19 age where Princeton researchers (2014) found that voting has little to no influence on policy in comparison to oligarchical monetary agendas. This goes to show we can and must restructure everything, so that we can stop propelling towards an inhabitable climate apocalypse.

From a critical media ecological standpoint these are "differences in media, and humans *as* media, that make differences", and why we require strikes and mutual aid coalitions -- ASAP.

We have the people power, well documented reasons, and drive to make enormous, fast changes. It just requires an orientational shift and understanding of *why* we're here and *what* to do next. That is already well under way, and we cannot fumble this opportunity to redeem autistic folks.

We need to acknowledge, and act from a critical ecological view, that all of this is connected. We must listen to disenfranchised members of our communities to direct actions, protecting all of us. Most millennials and Gen Z truly cannot afford to live now and see that we must make changes. The concept and reality of billionaires who've monopolized every industry must come to an end. We can't continue in this system that exploits, sickens, disables, and kills us for only their profit.

More days than not in the last 3 years Twinkle meows me out of my "bed rot." But now, I care for myself. And, after everything I've experienced and shared here, I know we all deserve better.

I am just one little bird flying a little route around the Midwest, so I couldn't possibly have seen all the map. Lucky for us -- the point of this isn't to grand stage me a single hero like every piece of colonial capitalist propaganda does! The point is that we need each other to survive. And we need to embrace a form of humanness most of us haven't been afforded by these establishments. Not that we need that, necessarily, to understand our own humanness, but we do deserve systems that acknowledge our humanness for the first time. And we can build them, so why wouldn't we?

Printed in the USA
CPSIA information can be obtained
at www.ICGtesting.com
LVHW051256270724
786681LV00010B/588